AF600045

THE CATHOLIC UNIVERSITY OF AMERICA
CANON LAW STUDIES
No. 192

EXTRA-JUDICIAL PROCURATORS IN THE CODE OF CANON LAW

BY THE

REV. CHARLES PAUL CONNORS, C.S.Sp., A.B., J.C.L.
Priest of the United States Province

A DISSERTATION

Submitted to the Faculty of the School of Canon Law of the Catholic University of America in Partial Fulfillment of the Requirements for the Degree of Doctor of Canon Law

THE CATHOLIC UNIVERSITY OF AMERICA PRESS, INC.
WASHINGTON, D. C.
1944

Nihil Obstat:

Clemens V. Bastnagel, J.U.D.,
Censor Deputatus.
Washingtonii, D. C., die 6 maii 1944.

Imprimi Potest:

Georgius I. Collins, C.S.Sp.,
Praepositus Provincialis.
Washingtonii, D. C., die 8 maii 1944.

Imprimatur:

✠Michael I. Curley, D.D.,
Archiepiscopus Baltimorensis-Washingtonensis.
Baltimorae, Md., die 11 maii 1944.

TO

MY MOTHER

TABLE OF CONTENTS

Page

PART ONE

EXTRA-JUDICIAL PROCURATORS IN GENERAL

CHAPTER I

CHAPTER II

PART TWO

THE USE OF EXTRA-JUDICIAL PROCURATORS

CHAPTER I

FOREWORD

Any system of laws, if it is to be complete, must provide its subjects with a rule of action that can be applied not merely in ordinary but in extraordinary cases as well. The law-maker in drawing up legislation seeks to establish a guide to be followed in every conceivable contingency.

The present work deals with what might be termed an emergency measure of canon law; for a procurator, or proxy, supplies the place of another and acts for that other. Since such a procedure is to be resorted to only extraordinarily in extra-judicial matters, one might be tempted to dismiss the subject of extra-judicial procurators as of too little importance to be considered at any great length. But the student of canon law must be as well acquainted with those provisions of the Church's legislation which are but seldom, even rarely, applied, as with provisions which are subject to daily application.

Moreover, the practice of appointing procurators has given rise, as this work will attempt to show, to various canonical offices which are now of such importance that they receive special consideration in the Church's legislation. Hence a knowledge of the origin and nature of the procurator's function will be an invaluable aid in arriving at a proper understanding of those offices which resulted from the frequent use of procurators in times past. Even secular law has felt the influence of the employment of proxies.

It is for all of these reasons that the subject of extra-judicial procurators is worthy of study.

The writer takes this occasion to express his gratitude to the superiors and members of the United States Province of the Congregation of the Holy Ghost and of the Immaculate Heart of Mary, for the opportunity of pursuing graduate study in canon law; to the faculty of the School of Canon Law of the Catholic University of America for their assistance and guidance, and to those who have, by supplying material and, above all, by displaying their interest and encouragement, aided in the preparation of this work.

INTRODUCTION

Procurators in General

The name, "procurator," though familiar enough, may have a connotation of perhaps no especial importance. The synonym, "proxy," is of more common usage. Certainly the function of a procurator is familiar enough, although the name may not be. For a procurator, as the etymology of the word indicates (*pro alio curator*), is, in the language of Bernard of Pavia (†1213), "is qui suscipit alienum negotium ministrandum mandato generali vel speciali."[1] Thus anyone authorized to act for another can, in a broad sense, be called a procurator.

It is true that this, then, is a very general term. Such it is by definition, and such it was in practise in the early days of the Church. Thus Pope Urban II (1088-1099), writing in the year 1088 to Lucinus, archdeacon of the Church of St. Vincent in Pavia, repeated the condemnation of simony issued by the Council of Chalcedon.[2] In this condemnation the Council spoke of "oeconomum vel defensorem." Pope Urban II, quoting the Council as speaking of "procuratorem vel defensorem," explained: "In nomine procuratoris intelligit praefata sinodus quemlibet ecclesisticarum rerum administratorem ut, verbi gratia, praepositum, oeconomum, vicedominum."[3] This letter of Pope Urban II is incorporated in the second part of the *Decretum Gratiani.*[4]

---

[1] *Summa Decretalium* (ed. E. A. Th. Layspeyres, Ratisbonae, 1860), lib. I, tit. XXIX, *de procuratoribus,* n. 1. This work will hereinafter be cited as *Summa.* The same concept was held in Roman law: "Procurator est qui aliena negotia mandatu domini administrat."—D. (3.3) 1.

[2] Can. 2—Mansi, *Sacrorum Conciliorum Nova et Amplissima Collectio* (53 voll. in 59, Parisiis, 1901-1927), VII, 393. This collection will hereinafter be referred to as Mansi.

[3] Jaffé, *Regesta Romanorum Pontificum* (2. ed., 2 voll., Lipsiae, 1885-1888), n. 5743; Mansi, XX, 661; Migne, *Patrologiae Cursus Completus, Series Latina* (221 voll., Parisiis, 1844-1864), CLI, 529. The work of Jaffé will hereinafter be cited by his name and that of Migne by the letters *MPL.*

[4] C. 8, C. I, q. 3.

The glossator of the *Extravagantes* of Pope John XXII (1316-1334), Zenzelinus de Cassanis († c. 1350), likewise made the term all-inclusive.[5]

This general term was reducible, for particular types of authorization, to a more specific nomenclature and was eventually replaced by it, thus accounting, in part at least, for the unfamiliarity of the title.[6] Thus an assistant priest in a parish, when acting in place of the pastor, could in this general sense be called a parochial procurator. But the more specific title of assistant pastor is better known and its use more natural.

Indeed, the very origin of the position of procurator is natural, arising, as it does, out of necessity. If human affairs are to be conducted efficiently, there must be a division of authority and execution, greater in proportion as the scope of the office widens. Thus even in civil affairs a minor official may perform all of his duties personally, but one in a position of greater responsibility must allocate his duties and authority to subordinates. As the Digest notes, in the conclusion of the passage cited above, the employment of procurators is absolutely necessary in order that those who are unwilling or unable to look after their own affairs may do so through others.

Types of Procurators

So it was that Roman law, despite the rigid formalism of its early period, later admitted the use of procurators in almost every branch of its application. Even in litigations, where the axiom was: "Nemo alieno nomine lege agere potest,"[7] the use of the procurator became of such importance that he received the specific designation of *procurator ad litem*. In commenting on this development, Hogan writes:

> Historical indications point to the early procurator as a *procurator omnium bonorum*, a universal partrimonial adminis-

[5] "Nomen procuratoris comprehendit sub se omnia nomina per quae quis alienae administrationi se poterit ingerere."—C. un., *ne sede vacante aliquid innovetur*, tit. V, in Extravag. Joan. XXII, *glossa* ad v. "vicariatus nomen."

[6] Cf. *infra*, p. 19.

[7] D. (50. 17) 123.

strator. In this capacity he would interest himself in all the affairs and negotiations of his principal, including actions. Gradually, however, it became necessary to designate a *procurator* specifically *ad lites.*[8]

A full treatment of this type of procurator in canon law may be found in Hogan's work. It is with the extra-judicial procurator, or *procurator ad negotia,* that the present study is exclusively concerned.

Even in regard to the latter type, a further division may be made. For a principal may assign to his agent the management of all his affairs (*procurator ad omnia*) or of some (*ad aliqua*) or even of one affair.[9] Despite some indications to the contrary, apparently Roman law recognized this last form of appointment.[10]

[8] *Judicial Advocates And Procurators,* The Catholic University of America Canon Law Studies, n. 133 (Washington, D. C.: The Catholic University of America Press, 1941), p. 14.

Buckland goes even so far as to say that this was the first use of the title for a specific rather than a general agent: "The mandate might be general, the management of the principal's affairs, the holder of such a mandate being properly called a procurator, though in the late classical law this name is applied to mandataries for a single service, the earliest application of it in this sense to a *procurator ad litem."—A Text-Book of Roman Law* (2. ed., Cambridge: The University Press, 1932), p. 514. Cf. Maynz, *Cours de Droit Romain* (3. ed., 3 vols., Paris, 1870-1874), II, 230-231.

[9] Cf. *glossa,* c. 1, *de procuratoribus,* I, 19, in VI°, ad v. "ad negotia."

[10] ". . . quamvis quidam, ut Pomponius libro vicesimo quarto scribit, non putent unius rei mandatum suscipientem procuratorem esse . . . sed verius est eum quoque procuratorem esse qui ad unam rem datus sit."—D. (3.3) 1. Cf. D. (46.7) (3.2): "sive huius rei tantum;" D. (46.3) 12.

Observes Albertario: "La funzione postclassica del mandato e della procura ha fatto sorgere accanto al *procurator,* cioè al *procurator omnium bonorum* o *ad res administrandas datus,* il *procurator unius rei.* Per modo che ciò che sarebbe stato un non senso per un giurista classico (l'esistenza di un *procurator unius rei* era un non senso nè più nè meno come l'esistenza di un mandatario generale) diventa nel diritto romano-bizantino una cosa possibile e ovvia."—*Procurator Unius Rei* (Pavia, 1921), p. 2.

PART ONE

EXTRA-JUDICIAL PROCURATORS IN GENERAL

CHAPTER I

General Principles Governing The Use Of Procurators

As is the case with every canonical institution, an understanding of the function of a procurator must be based on a knowledge of its historical development. Indeed, such a knowledge is especially necessary in this matter, because in the course of time the importance of the role of procurator as such has declined considerably, and consequently little of the legislation pertaining to it is of recent origin. Whereas three collections of decretals contained in the *Corpus Iuris Canonici* devote separate titles to the subject of procurators in general,[1] the Code of Canon Law nowhere gives special consideration to the subject, although it does contain one chapter on judicial procurators and advocates.[2] Hence for most of the general principles involved it is necessary to revert to the older collections.

The fundamental principles underlying the use of procurators are set down in the *Regulae Juris. Regula 68* states: "Potest quis per alium quod potest facere per seipsum." To this, as to most general principles, are to be found exceptions, some of which will be considered later. Suffice it to say for the moment that these exceptions may arise either from the nature of the case or from positive law; but the exception is to be demonstrated.[3]

---

[1] Lib. I, tit. 38, of the Decretals of Gregory IX; lib. I, tit. 19, of the *Liber Sextus* of Boniface VIII; and lib. I, tit. 10, of the Clementine Collection.

[2] Lib. IV, tit. IV, c. II; cans. 1655-1666.

[3] The same principle is enunciated in Roman law: "Cum quaeritur an alicui procuratorem habere liceat, inspiciendum erit an non prohibeatur procuratorem dare, quia hoc edictum prohibitorium est."—D. (3.3) 43.

As Reiffenstuel (1641-1703) summed up: "In omnibus negotiis et causis potest intervenire procurator, in quibus non reperitur expresse prohibitum."—*Ius Canonicum Universum* (5 voll. in 4, Venetiis, 1735), lib. I, tit. XXXVIII, n. 59.

In general, then, it is not required that everything one does he do personally. On the contrary, the use of another as a medium in the performance of many actions is perfectly legitimate. Hence the principle that one can do through others what one can do one's self.

The contrary of this rule is equally true; that is, he who cannot act for himself cannot act through another.[4] Thus an infant cannot have a procurator, but rather has a *curator* or guardian. An insane person is, in this regard, comparable to an infant.[5]

Article 1. The Authority of a Procurator

What authority inheres in actions performed by a procurator? Again there exists a *Regula Juris* as a guide: "Qui facit per alium est perinde ac si faciat per seipsum,"[6] for the procurator is looked upon as the principal himself.[7] This, indeed, is the basis for accepting a procurator at all. It is brought out with great emphasis by the glossator of the *Decretum Gratiani* in the matter of an oath: "Procurator iurat in animam domini."[8] Most decisive in its legalistic finality is the statement of Bernard of Pavia that the effect of procuratorship is that what is done by a procurator is to be accepted as done by the principal.[9]

Article 2. Qualifications

Certain requirements are made in regard to the fitness of those acting as procurators. Boniface VIII (1294-1303), in this matter, presumed the capability of the appointee and placed the bur-

[4] "Quod enim non possum per me, neque per alium."—*Glossa,* c. 10, D. XLVI, ad v. "aut inferendas." "Quis suo nomine exercere prohibetur id nec per subiectam personam agere debet."—D. (50.8) (2.1).

[5] C. 105, D. IV, *de cons.* Cf. can. 1648, § 1.

[6] Reg. 72, R.J., in VI°.

[7] "Il procurator era nell' antica società romana *quasi quidam paene dominus,* come Cicerone avverte, e non ripiteva dal mandato le sue funzioni. Era il *dominus* di fatto, in assenza e per l'assenza del *dominus* di diritto."—Albertario, *Procurator Unius Rei,* p. 23.

[8] *Glossa* of c. 33, D. LXIII, ad v. "et iurare."

[9] "Effectus procurationis est ut ratum sit quod geritur cum procuratore ac si domino gestum esset."—*Summa,* lib. I, tit. XXIX, *de procuratoribus,* n. 7.

den of proof on the one contesting his fitness.[10] Durandus [Duranti] (c. 1237-1296), before succinctly summarizing this principle in the words, "Quicumque non prohibetur, admittitur," asserted that one incapable of handling his own affairs was consequently incapable of handling another's as procurator.[11]. It requires no profound thought to see the logic of this, nor any great stretch of the imagination to see the possibility of its application. Thus an infant or an insane person is excluded from such an office, and a person who is incapable of understanding the mandate is barred from attempting to carry it out.

A. Age

A decretal of Boniface VIII established a minimum age of seventeen years for extra-judicial procurators and twenty-five years for judicial procurators.[12] Hostiensis (†1271), in commenting on the difference in the age requirement for judicial and extra-judicial procurators, claimed that the reason for this difference was evident, for the latter seeks a private good but the former the public good and hence has need of the greater prudence that age can be expected to bring.[13]

Because, according to some later commentators, the purpose of Boniface VIII in issuing this decretal was to set a minimum age for *procuratores ad iudicia,* and the reference to the age of *procuratores ad negotia* was only incidental, the age requirement for extra-judicial procurators was taken rather lightly. Thus Sanchez (1550-1610), although admitting that a more mature person should be appointed as procurator in certain affairs, claimed

10 "Regulariter, qui non prohibetur expresse ad exercendum procurationis officium idoneus debeat reputari."—C. 1, *de procuratoribus,* I, 19, in VI°. The chapter refers expressly to *procuratores ad litem;* but since glossators and commentators applied even more specific requirements given elsewhere for this type of procurator to *procuratores ad negotia* as well, the illation made here is valid.

11 *Speculum Iuris* (Venetiis, 1577), lib. I, partic. III, *de procuratore,* n. 1. Cf. Hostiensis, *Summa Aurea* (Venetiis, 1570), lib. I, tit. XXXVIII, *de procuratoribus,* n. 15; D. (3.3) 2.

12 C. 5, *de procuratoribus,* I, 19, in VI°. Cf. C. (2.12) 14. Although a *procurator ad negotia* could act in court trials, he could do so only when he had reached the age required of judicial procurators. Cf. D. (3.3) 51.

13 *In Libros Decretalium Commentaria* (3 voll., Venetiis, 1581), lib. I, tit. XXXVIIII, *de procuratoribus,* c. 14, n. 3.

that no particular age was required in a proxy for marriage, but only the quality that natural law demanded; that is, the use of reason.[14]

Later canonists followed Sanchez' view, employing the same argument.[15] Interpreting the aim of Boniface VIII's decretal to be the establishment of a minimum age for judicial procurators, Lombardi (†1908) concluded that the age mentioned for a "procurator ad negotia" is merely an indication of what is "decens."[16] Cappello, in his commentary on canons 1088 and 1089, states that no particular quality is required in a procurator who contracts marriage for another.[17] Indeed, this same conclusion can be made in regard to all procurators, in view of canon 6, 6°, [18] so that no specific age is required in a proxy, but only that he have the use of reason, unless the certainty of a proper execution of the mandate or the natural demand of a proper juridical decorum require one of a more mature age.

B. Legal Status

Besides the natural abilities of the one chosen as procurator, there is to be considered his status before the law.

1. Juridically Infamous Persons

A strong argument might be made to show that juridic infamy

---

[14] *De Sancto Matrimonii Sacramento* (Antverpiae, 1626), lib. III, disp. XLI, n. 8.

[15] Cf. Ferraris, *Prompta Bibliotheca, Canonica, Iuridica, Moralis, Theologica, necnon Ascetica, Polemica, Rubricistica, Historica* (9 voll., Romae, 1885-1899), VI, 458, sub. v. "procurator", n. 42; Wernz, *Ius Decretalium* (6 voll., Romae, 1898-1905), IV, 45. Ferraris' work will hereinafter be referred to as *Bibliotheca.*

[16] "De Matrimonio Per Procuratorem, Nuncium, Interpretem, Litteras, Telegraphum et Telephonum"—*Acta Sanctae Sedis* (41 voll., Romae 1865-1908), XXXVIII (1905-1906), 189. This article will hereinafter be referred to as "De Matrimonio Per Procuratorem." The *Acta* will be indicated by the initials, *ASS.*

[17] *Tractatus Canonico-Moralis de Sacramentis* (vol. I, 2. ed. emendata et aucta, Taurinorum Augustae: Officina Libraria Marietti, 1928; vol. III, 4. ed. emendata et aucta, Taurinorum Augustae: Officina Libraria Marietti, 1939), III, n. 619, 2°.

[18] "Si qua ex ceteris disciplinaribus legibus, quae usque adhuc viguerunt, nec explicite nec implicite in Codice contineatur, ea vim omnem amisisse dicenda est."

(infamia iuris) would exclude one from validly performing the duties of a procurator, even *ante sententiam*. In the *Decretum Gratiani* it is explicitly stated: "Infamis persona nec procurator esse potest, nec cognitor."[19] The gloss refers to the canon pointing out that since bishops and priests are to work for the glory of God they must choose as their vice-gerents only those who enjoy a good reputation.[20] The argument might proceed to show that this legislation is embodied in canon 2294, § 1: "Qui infamia iuris laborat . . . est inhabilis ad obtinenda beneficia, pensiones, officia, et dignitates ecclesiasticas, ad actus legitimos ecclesiasticos perficiendos, ad exercitium iuris aut muneris ecclesiastici . . ." But the function of a procurator in the Church is a "munus ecclesiasticum."[21]

This argument, however, is refuted on the following grounds:

1. The canons cited from Gratian are applied by commentators to procurators of ecclesiastics exclusively. Thus Panormitanus [Nicholas de Tudeschis] (1386-1445) stated that unless he was acting for a bishop, one who was laboring under juridic infamy could still serve as a *procurator ad negotia*.[22] Pirhing (1606-1679) held that this prohibition affected all procurators acting for ecclesiastical persons, but not those acting for lay people.[23]

2. While it is true that canon 2294, § 1, renders those afflicted with the penalty of infamy incapable of exercising an ecclesiastical function, it has the same effect in regard to legal ecclesiastical actions. Among these, as enumerated in canon 2256,

---

19 C. 1, C. III, q. 7.

20 C. 3, C. V, q. 3. It is interesting to note that whereas the canon itself says: "debet unusquisque eorum . . . habere advocatum non malae famae suspecti sed bonae opinionis," the gloss (ad v. "advocatum") explains: "id est, procuratorem."

21 Cf. *infra*, p. 20.

22 *Commentaria in Quinque Decretalium Libros* (8 voll., Venetiis, 1588), lib. I, tit. VII, *de iuramento calumniae*, c. 4, n. 9. Cf. Cencius, *Tractatus De Procuratoribus* (opus posthumum a Petro Hyeronimo Cencio adauctum et illustratum, Florentiae, 1857), p. 103, c. XXII, n. 2.

23 "Infames infamia iuris vel facti iure canonico ad officium procuratoris sive ad lites sive etiam ad negotia pro ecclesiasticis personis non admittuntur sed pro laicis tantum."—*Ius Canonicum in Quinque Libris Decretalium* (5 voll. in 4, Dilingae, 1677), lib. I, tit. XXXVIII, n. 23.

2° are: "munus patrini agere in sacramentis baptismi et confirmationis; suffragium ferre in electionibus ecclesiasticis." Yet this is expressly made to apply only *post sententiam* in the following canons:

Can. 765—Ut quis sit patrinus [in baptismo] oportet: . . .

2° Ad nullam pertineat haereticam aut schismaticam sectam, nec sententia condemnatoria vel declaratoria sit excommunicatus aut infamis infamia iuris aut exclusus ab actibus legitimis . . .

Can. 766—Ut autem quis licite patrinus [in baptismo] admittatur, oportet: . . .

2° Non sit propter notorium delictum excommunicatus vel exclusus ab actibus legitimis vel infamis infamia iuris, quin tamen sententia intercesserit. . .

Can. 795—Ut quis sit patrinus [in confirmatione] oportet:...

2° Nulli haereticae aut schismaticae sectae sit adscriptus, nec ulla ex poenis de quibus in can. 765, n. 2 per sententiam declaratoriam aut condemnatoriam notatus.

Can. 796—Ut quis licite patrini munus [in confirmatione] admittatur, oportet: . . .

3° Serventur . . . praescripta can. 766.

Can. 167—Nequeunt suffragium ferre [in electione]: . . .

3° Censura vel infamia iuris affecti, post sententiam tamen declaratoriam vel condemnatoriam . . .

Hence, although canon 2294, § 1, states that those penalized with juridic infamy are incapable of exercising legal ecclesiastical acts, and canon 2256, 2°, enumerates among such acts sponsorship in baptism and confirmation and voting in an election, the above-cited canons dealing with these acts expressly declare that they are invalid only when they are performed by a penalized person *post sententiam*; otherwise, they are merely illicit.

The same conclusion can be made in regard to procurators by the application of Canon 20.[24]

[24] "Si certa de re desit expressum praescriptum legis sive generalis sive particularis, norma sumeda est . . . a legibus latis in similibus; a generalibus iuris principiis cum aequitate canonica servatis . . . "

2. *Excommunicated Persons*

An excommunicated person would likewise act illicitly as proxy, but invalidly only if a declaratory or condemnatory sentence had been pronounced on his excommunication; for canon 2265 reads as follows:

§ 1 Quilibet excommunicatus:...

2° Nequit consequi dignitates . . . aliudve munus in Ecclesia;

§ 2 Actus tamen positus contra praescriptum § 1, nn. 1, 2, non est nullus, nisi positus fuerit ab excommunicato vitando vel ab alio excommunicato post sententiam declaratoriam vel condemnatoriam...[25]

3. *Non-Catholics*

May a non-Catholic validly act as proxy in ecclesiastical matters? Yes, as long as he is not excluded on other grounds; for nowhere in the Code is membership in the Church made a requisite for the validity of carrying out a mandate, even in connection with the reception of some of the sacraments. Nor need there be any distinction made between baptized and unbaptized non-Catholics (except where a declaratory or condemnatory sentence is had against a baptized non-Catholic) since the same applies to both categories.[26]

However, the admission of such persons as procurators would be gravely illicit, and hence permissible only for a very grave reason. It is gravely illicit from the divine law since it is an active participation by a non-Catholic in the rites of the Church. Then, too, the possibility of scandal may be present. If, for example, a non-Catholic were proxy for a Catholic sponsor in baptism, the erroneous impression might be gained that the non-Catholic was the sponsor. This, of course, is strictly forbidden.[27]

---

[25] Can. 2263 states: "... excommunicatus . . . prohibetur ecclesiasticis officiis seu muneribus fungi."

[26] Cf. Cappello, *De Sacramentis*, III, n. 619, 2°; *infra*, p. 38, note [31].

[27] Can. 765, 1°, 2°.

Article 3. The Mandate

A. Formalities

In the appointment of procurators formerly no particular formalities were necessary as long as the fact of appointment could be verified. If a written mandate was used, the document gave the names of the principal and the agent, the nature of the matter to be undertaken and the principal's promise, implied if not expressed, of the ratification of the acts of the procurator. These letters were to be rendered authentic by the use of one's private seal or the testimony of a notary or witness.[28] The glossator of the Clementine Decretals noted that this was a case in which "littera et sigillum privati facit fidem."[29]

While the commentators spoke only of the written appointment of procurators, merely vocal authorization was not excluded as long as such authorization could be proved. As a general principle, and exclusive of any provisions to the contrary, writing was not necessary for the validity of any contract.[30]

Formerly no exception was made even in the matter of marriage.[31] Hence the use of an oral mandate was admitted as valid

---

[28] Durandus, *Speculum Iuris*, lib. I, partic. III, *de procuratore*, § 4, n. 9; Hostiensis, *Commentaria*, lib. I, tit. XXXVIII, *de procuratorbius*, c. 1; Panormitanus, *Commentaria*, lib. I, tit. XXXVIII, *de procuratoribus*, c. 1.

[29] *Glossa* of c. 1, I, *de procuratoribus*, 10, in Clem., ad v. "vel litteris."

[30] "Donatio et quilibet alius contractus solo partium consensu perficitur, quia seclusa partium conventione, scriptura magis ad probationem quam ad perfectionem contractus requiritur."—*Sanctae Rotae Romanae Decisiones coram Molines* (5 voll., Romae, 1728), V, 383, dec. MCCLIII, 4 apr. 1710, n. 17. "Nam in iurisdictionali est necessaria scriptura . . . in mandato autem ad negocia non requiritur scriptura."—Cencio, *De Procuratoribus*, c. XXVI, n. 14.

[31] Cf. Sanchez, *De Sancto Matrimonii Sacramento*, lib. II, disp. XI, n. 14; Gutierrez, *Quaestiones Canonicae* (3 voll., Noribergae, 1647), lib. III, c. XLIII, n. 16; Berardi, *Theologia Moralis* (5 voll., Faventiae, 1905), V, n. 1041; Lombardi, "De Matrimonio Per Procuratorem"—*ASS* XXXVIII (1905-1906), 189; *infra*, p. 41.

even in such cases.[32] In fact, the Sacred Congregation of the Council admitted the validity of a mandate given orally to a proxy for a sponsor in the sacrament of confirmation since matrimony, a sacrament having even graver legal consequences than confirmation, could be contracted through a proxy having only an oral mandate.[33]

Although an exception has been made by the Code in the matter of proxy marriage,[34] in general an oral mandate is still sufficient for the valid appointment of a procurator. Despite the stringent measures it contains, a recent instruction of the Sacred Congregation of the Sacraments in regard to the use of proxies for sponsors in the sacraments of baptism and confirmation does not demand that a written mandate be given when the authenticity of the appointment can be otherwise ascertained.[35]

B. Limits

Upon the acceptance of an authentic mandate, then, the procurator is empowered to act.

In the older legislation the mandate could be of a general nature, thus constituting the recipient a *procurator ad omnia;* or of a specific nature, for this or that affair. In practise, today, however, the general mandate can be disregarded in extrajudicial affairs, except in the matter of contracts, since a procurator must prove the authenticity of his mandate for each particular act.[36] When there is question of contracts, the civil law is to be

---

[32] S. C. C., *Neapolitana,* 7 apr. 1883—*ASS,* XVI (1883), 10-27; Sacra Romana Rota, *Tergestina,* 28 ian. 1931—*Sacrae Romanae Rotae Decisiones seu Sententiae* (Romae, 1909—), XXIII (1931), 27. This latter collection will hereinafter be referred to as *SRR. Dec.*

[33] *Nucerina,* 11 iun. 1881—*Thesaurus Resolutionum Sacrae Congregationis Concilii* (167 voll., Romae, 1718-1908), CXL (1881), 409.

[34] Can. 1089, §§ 1 and 2; cf. *infra,* pp. 40-42.

[35] S. C. de Sacramentis, 24 iul. 1925—*Acta Apostolicae Sedis, Commentarium Officiale* (Romae, 1909—), XVIII (1926), 44-47. Hereinafter this organ will be referred to by the initials *AAS.* Cf. *infra,* p. 26.

[36] The judicial procurator is still required, by canon 1659, to have a "speciale mandatum ad lites scriptum." Moreover, the attorney-at-law must have a special mandate before he can validly take various measures on behalf of his principal. Cf. cans. 1662; 1740, § 2.

followed[37] and hence a general mandate can be issued, constituting the recipient a general agent.

Even in the older legislation, because of the gravity of their nature and their consequences, for some matters a special mandate was required by positive law; so that, although the procurator had been authorized for all things, a still further authorization was necessary to handle matters thus reserved.[38] Examples of such reservation were the contracting of marriage,[39] the taking of an oath,[40] etc.

Furthermore, a principal cannot assign to his procurator greater power than he himself enjoys. Thus the philosophical axiom, "nemo dat quod non habet," can be stated in legal terms: "nemo plus iuris ad alium transferre potest, quam ipse haberet."[41]

In the event that a procurator exceeds the limits of his mandate, his act is invalid. Thus Innocent III (1198-1216), writing in the year 1209 to the bishops of Paris and Troyes and the abbot of St. Genevieve, declared null a sentence of excommunication rendered by a delegated judge, because that official had overstepped the bounds of his authority as set forth in the rescript of his appointment; for, asserted the pontiff, a procurator has authority only in those matters expressed in his commission.[42]

---

[37] Can. 1529.

[38] C. 1, 4, 5, *de procuratoribus,* I, 19, in VI°; c. 2, *de procuratoribus,* I, 10, in Clem. For the special mandate in Roman law, cf. D. (2.2) (3.1); (3.3) 63; (4.4) (25.1); (23.2) 34; (47.10) (17.16).

[39] C. 9, *de procuratoribus,* I, 19, in VI°. D. (23.2) 34 reads: "Generali mandato quaerendi mariti filiae familias non fieri nuptias rationis est." While this does not refer to proxy marriage, it may well be argued that *a fortiori* a special mandate was required even in Roman law for such a marriage.

[40] C. 4, *de procuratoribus,* I, 19, in VI°; *glossa* of Reg. 68, R. J., in VI°. Cf. Durandus, *Speculum Iuris,* lib. I, partic. III, *de procuratore,* § 1, n. 6; Hostiensis, *Commentaria,* lib. I, tit. VI, *de electione et postestate electi,* n. 62; D. (12.2) (17.3).

[41] D. (50.17) 54.

[42] "Procurator ad illa solummodo intelligatur constitutus quae in commissionis litteris inveniuntur expressa."—C. 32, X, *de officio et potestate iudicis delegati,* I, 29; *Regesta Pontificum Romanorum* (2 voll., ed. Augustus Potthast, Berolini, 1874-1875), n. 3663. The last-named work will hereinafter be designated by the editor's name.

"Si procurator ad unam speciem constitutus officium mandati egressus est, id quod gessit nullum praeiudicium facere potuit."—C. (2.12) 10.

The glossator of the Gregorian Decretals remarked: "Videtur quod si procurator fines mandati excedit, domino sciente, praeiudicet domino nisi statim contradicat."[43] He drew a parallel with a statement of Alexander III (1159-1181) to the bishop of Norwich to the effect that if a prelate alienated temporal goods belonging to a chapter, "conventu sciente et non contradicente," the act was to be held valid.[44]

A procurator who acted without a special mandate in a matter that required one, thereby exceeded the limits of his authority and did not bind him whom he represented. Instead, he himself was held to the consequences.[45]

From the very nature of the case, since a principal should be responsible for the actions of his representative only insofar as the latter has been authorized to act, and in view of canon 203, § 1,[46] —for procuratorship closely parallels delegation—[47] this principle still holds true by the application of canon 20.[48]

C. *Substitution and the Mandate*

The mandate can further restrict the power of the procurator by forbidding him to appoint another to act in his place. This restriction must be expressed, for the general rule would permit extra-judicial procurators to depute others.[49] An exception is had

---

[43] *Glossa* ad v. "protinus contradixit."

[44] C. 2, X, *de his quae fiunt a praelatis sine consensu capituli,* III, 10; Jaffé, n. 14033.

[45] *Casus* in c. 4, *de procuratoribus,* I, 19, in VI°, *in fine.* "Diligenter igitur fines mandati custodiendi sunt; nam qui excessit aliud quid facere videtur et, si susceptum non impleverit, tenetur."—D. (17.1) 5, Cf. C. (17.1) 41.

[46] "Delegatus qui sive circa res sive circa personas mandati sui fines excedit, nihil agit."

[47] Cf. *infra,* pp. 19-20.

[48] "Si certa de re desit expressum praescriptum legis . . . norma sumenda est . . . a legibus latis in similibus . . ."

[49] C. 1, *de procuratoribus,* I, 19, in VI°, reads: "Procurator datus ad negotia potest libere quandocumque alium deputare." The preceding paragraph of the same chapter permits substitution to a procurator *ad iudicia* only "post litem contestatam." Canon 1656, § 1, rules: "Unicum quisque potest eligere procuratorem, qui nequit alium sibimet substituere, nisi expressa facultas eidem facta fuerit."

in the contracting of marriage by proxy, where no substitution is permitted.[50] Prior to the code this same exception existed. The principal, however could give the procurator authority to depute another, but this had to be expressed.[51]

D. Plural Procuration and the Mandate

The *Corpus Iuris Canonici* permitted the appointment of several procurators for the same service. If all were appointed jointly, they had to act as a unit; the separate acts of any one were otherwise null. If, however, they were appointed *in solidum,* then any one of these could carry out the transaction, but the preference was accorded to him who first undertook the affair, and the others were without authority, unless for some reason the first failed to complete his task.[52]

E. Cessation of the Mandate

The *Corpus Iuris Canonici* states the causes for the cessation of the procurator's mandate. Besides being terminated with the execution of the mandated task, the mandate ceased to have force in five cases; namely, in the cases of

a) death of the principal;
b) death of the procurator;
c) revocation;
d) renunciation;
e) expiration of the time fixed for the execution of the mandate.

a) The following chapter, the basis of which is found in Roman law,[53] is contained in the Clementine Decretals:

---

[50] Can. 1089, § 4.

[51] C. 9, *de procuratoribus,* I, 19, in VI°. The chapter mentioned that this was not true of other cases of procuratorship.

[52] C. 14, X, *de procuratoribus,* I, 38; c. 6, *de procuratoribus,* I, 19, in VI°; Reg. 54, R. J., in VI° ("Qui prior est tempore, potior est iure"); Durandus, *Speculum Iuris,* lib. I, partic. III, *de procuratore,* n. 3. The source of this principle is found in D. (3.3) 32: "Pluribus procuratoribus in solidum simul datis, occupantis melior condicio erit, ut posterior non sit in eo quod prior petit procurator."

[53] "Inter causas omittendi mandati mors mandatoris est: nam mandatum solvitur morte."—D. (17.1) 26.

> Procuratorem a praelato rectore vel alio quolibet pro ecclesia sua vel beneficio constitutum, per mortem constituentis revocari censemus etiam quoad negotia iam incepta, et causas in quibus per ipsum lis fuerit ante mortem huiusmodi contesta.[54]

b) As regards the death of the procurator, Hostiensis, considering both parties of the relationship, wrote that a mandate is terminated by the death of either the principal or the agent.[55]

c) A constitution of Clement V (1305-1314), incorporated in the Clementine Decretals, ruled that a renunciation of any dignity or benefice made through a procurator took effect, even though the principal had revoked the mandate prior to its execution, if at the time of the renunciation neither the agent nor the authority accepting it was aware of the revocation. An exception was made if knowledge of the revocation was kept from either of these parties by evil design.[56] Knowledge of the revocation, then, on the part of either the procurator or the third party, was necessary and sufficient, as the glossators of the above decretal[57] and of the Decretals of Gregory IX noted.[58]

The same was not true of the judicial procurator, for in such a case revocation had to be made known to the adversaries and the judge, so that if the procurator himself was aware of the revoca-

---

[54] C. 4, *de procuratoribus,* I, 10, in Clem. The glossator notes (ad. v. "negotia"): "Credo quod intendit per hoc designare procuratorem negotiorum et per verba sequentia procuratorem iudiciorum." Cf. c. un., *de renunciatione,* I, 4, in Clem., *glossa* ad v. "quomodolibet."

[55] *Commentaria,* lib. II, tit. XXII, *de fide instrumentorum,* c. 2, n. 5. The Institutes of Gaius read: "Si adhuc integro mandato mors alterius interveniat; id est, vel eius qui mandarit vel eius qui mandatum susceperit, solvitur mandatum."—III, 160. Cf. D. (17.1) (27.3).

[56] C. un., *de renunciatione,* I, 4, in Clem. Cf. *glossa* of C. 33, D. LXIII, ad v. "et iurare" for the same prescription in regard to an oath by proxy. Roman law embodied the same principle in D. (17.1) 15; (15.4) 2. Canon 186 permits the renunciation of any ecclesiastical office to be made by proxy and cites the above chapter of the Clementine Decretals as a source.

[57] *Glossa* ad v. "ignorantem."

[58] "Extra iudicium . . . sufficit quod revocatio perveniat ad procuratorem et postea non valet quod facit in praeiudicium domini sed bene valet quod facit antequam revocatio ad eum perveniat."—C. 33, X, *de rescriptis,* I, 3, *glossa* ad v. "propter suspicionem."

tion, and not the others, the principal was still held to the acts of his agent.[59]

The exception in regard to marriage was a matter of actual legislation [60] and is still the law.[61]

d) The procurator was free to renounce his function through the legal principle that an obligation can be terminated by the same cause by which it was created.[62] Of course, if the procurator had already begun to execute the mandate, he could not forsake it to the disadvantage of the principal.[63]

e) If a time was fixed within which the mandate was to be executed, the expiration of the time rendered an unexcuted mandate null, for this was equivalent to a necessary condition.[64]

Because they flow from general principles, these causes of the cessation of the mandate—death, revocation, renunciation and the expiration of the time fixed—are applicable even today.[65] An additional cause of cessation, the subsequent insanity of the principal, peculiar to a mandate to contract marriage for another, is established by the Code of Canon Law.[66]

---

[59] C. 33, X, *de rescriptis,* I, 3.

[60] C. 9, *de procuratoribus,* I, 19, in VI°.

[61] Can. 1089, § 3.

[62] C. 1, X, *de regulis iuris,* V, 41. Roman law expressed it: "Nihil tam naturale est quam eo genere quidque dissolvere, quo colligatum est."—D. (50.17) 35.

[63] "Si quis absentis negotia gesserit, si quidem ex mandatu, palam est ex contractu nasci inter eos actiones mandati, quibus invicem experiri possunt de eo, quod alterum alteri ex bona fide praestare oportet."—D. (44.7) 5. Thus a contract was established. Consequently the matter of revocation and reunciation are treated together. Cf. D. (3.3) 19-24; (17.1) (27.2).

[64] Thus Alexander III wrote to the bishop-elect of Chartres: "De causis, quae infra certum terminum decidendae committuntur, hoc tuam volumus cognitionem tenere, quod, nisi dies praefixus de communi consensu partium prorogetur, eo transacto, mandatum expirat."—C. 4, X, de *officio et potestate iudicis delegati,* I, 29. It is true that this response referred to judicial proceedings, but the nature of the case warrants its application to all mandates.

[65] Cf. can. 207 for causes of the cessation of delegated power.

[66] Can. 1089, § 3. Cf. *infra,* pp. 43-44.

CHAPTER II

NATURE OF THE EXTRA-JUDICIAL PROCURATOR'S FUNCTION

The contrast between the abundance and detail of the legislation and commentary on the subject of extra-judicial procurators during the period of the *Corpus Iuris Canonici* and the period following it, and the little attention paid to the same subject in the Code of Canon Law raises two questions, seemingly unrelated to each other but in reality to be answered together.

1. How is it that this subject occupied so important a position in the earlier collections of canon law, and yet today receives apparently only incidental treatment in canonical legislation?

2. What is the nature of the function of the procurator?

For the answers to these questions the definition of a procurator as cited above may be recalled:[1] "is qui suscipit alienum negotium ministrandum mandato generali vel speciali." Comment was made on this definition to the effect that any one authorized to act for another could, in a broad sense, be called a procurator. Actually, for some time in the Church the term was used in this broad sense, applied to any agent acting for another and in another's name.[2]

---

[1] P. viii.

[2] Hammond, in his notes to Blackstone's Commentaries, attributes the origin of the institution of agency in secular law to the corresponding institution in canon law, and points out the extensive field in which it operates. "The law of principal and agent is derived from the canon law and has only been introduced into the common law in recent times. If the older books of English law are examined no such words as principal and agent will be found in them. Whenever any question is discussed which would now be treated under that head, it is treated of as master and servant . . . Agency" [has become] "the rubric under which almost everything is ranged that relates either to the contracts or the torts formed or committed by one person at the instance of another."—Blackstone, *Commentaries On The Laws Of England* (ed. with notes by William G. Hammond, 4 vols., San Francisco, 1890), I, 719; notes to Book I, ch. 14, sec. 432.

The term "agency" is just as broad in its application in secular law as the term "procuratorship" was formerly in canon law. "It is the general rule that agency may be created for the transaction of any lawful business and that whatever a person may lawfully do, if acting in his right and in his own behalf, he may lawfully delegate to an agent."—Mechem, *Outlines On Agency* (3. ed., Chicago: Callaghan and Co., 1923), p. 23, sec. 40.

It must be remembered that although our divine Saviour in founding the Church determined the fundamental character of its government, nevertheless He did not create *in specie* all the ecclestiastical offices that would, by reason of its growth geographically and numerically become necessary in the course of time.[3] The administrative needs of the Church, soon after its founding, demanded the apportioning of authority and duties and the employment of assistants. Many of the new tasks brought on by the Church's rapid growth were assigned to individuals representing him whose responsibilities they were; in other words, a procurator was appointed for all or for some such tasks or even for one specific task. These assistants eventually, by the very natural process of habitual practice, came to be, as it were, specialists, designated for particular functions; and their appointment in many cases led to the creation of permanent ecclesiastical offices, in which cases the individuals filling such offices would no longer be known as procurators, but by titles which designated, in some apt way, their status or functions.[4]

Fournier traces particularly the origin of the office of the vicar general to the use by bishops of general procurators in the early Church, originally in the absence of the bishop, but eventually even when he was present in his diocese.[5] This is contrary to the

---

[3] "Cum Ecclesia Christi magis magisque propagaretur, pro crescente in dies multitudine negotiorum novi administri episcopis omnino fuerunt necessarii."—Wernz, *Ius Decretalium,* II, n. 800.

[4] "A vrai dire, tous les prêtres, tous les diacres, tous les clercs de son église sont à degrés divers, les auxiliaires, les coopérateurs, les vicaires —au sens large—de l'évêque . . . Tous ces differents rouages sont apparus au cours des premiers siècles, se sont constitués et finalement moulés, pour ainsi dire, dans un type devenu classique. Au début ils étaient en dépendance très étroite et très intime du chef du diocèse, les utilisait a son gré, suivant les circonstances et les besoins. Peu à peu, leurs attributions se sont differenciées et hierarchisées devenant plus ou moins la propriété du titulaire"—Fournier, *Les Origines du Vicaire-Général* (Paris, 1922), pp. 32-33.

[5] *Les Origines du Vicaire-Général,* pp. 129-130. Cf. pp. 114-115; 120. The substitute for the bishop of Troyes during that prelate's visit to Constantinople is addressed by Innocent III in a letter of May 1, 1210, as "procurator generalis."—C. 25, X, *de praebendis et dignitatibus,* III, 5; Potthast, n. 3989. Cf. Dalpiaz' review of Fournier's work in *Apollinaris* (Romae, 1928—), II (1929), 523: "Congruenter ad eius originem vicarius generalis est iuridice constitutus secundum exemplar procuratoris romani."

hypothesis of the origin of the vicar-general's office as first advanced by Thomassinus, and accepted by all later canonists almost without exception. This author maintained that the office of vicar-general was created by the bishops of the twelfth century and almost universally established in the thirteenth century to off-set the excessive power of the archdeacon. He further claimed that there was no mention of the office of vicar-general in the *Decretum Gratiani* nor in the Decretals of Gregory IX.[6]

Fournier shows that up to about the eleventh century the immediate assistants of the bishops in both spiritual and temporal affairs were called "ministri" or "procuratores," the nature and extent of whose duties correspond to the nature and extent of the duties of the vicar-general today.[7] In the course of the eleventh century the term *"officiales"* was also used. This would explain a change of wording by the author of a *casus* in the *Liber Sextus.* Boniface VIII ruled:

> Cum . . . nec regulariter donare valeat is, cui bonorum administratio etiam libera est concessa: *officialis* aut *vicarius generalis* episcopi beneficia conferre non possunt, nisi beneficiorum collatio ipsis specialiter sit commissa.[8]

The *casus,* remarking the conclusions to be made from this ruling, has it:

[6] *Vetus et Nova Ecclesiae Disciplina* (10 voll., Magontiaci 1787), pars I, lib. II, c. 8, nn. 1-5.

[7] *Les Origines du Vicaire-Général,* p. 55. "Les premiers cadres juridiques certains, dans lesquels nous est apparu le vicaire-général, sont ceux de *procurator generalis.* Cette origine a conditionné tout le developpement ultérieur de l'institution, et en explique les particularités."—*Op. cit.,* p. 120. Whether or not this assertion of Fournier is admitted, there is no denying that the positions of the procurator and of the vicar general in relation to the bishop are closely parallel. The extent and duration of the authority of both depend on the bishop; both have need of special mandates in certain matters in addition to their general powers. Cf. cans. 336, § 2; 368, § 1; 371.

It is interesting to note that Du Cange *(Glossarium Mediae et Infimae Latinitatis,* conditum a Carolo Du Fresne Domino du Cange, auctum a Monachis Ordinis S. Benedicti cum supplementis integris D. P. Carpenterii, digessit G. A. L. Henschel, Vol. VI [Paris: Libraire des Sciences et des Arts, 1938], p. 521) gives as the meanings of *procurator,* "vicarius" and "locum tenens."

[8] C. 3, *de officio vicarii,* I, 13, in VI°.

> Nota quod *procurator* omnium bonorum cum libera administratione et generali potestate ut possit facere ea, quae constituens faceret, non potest dare bona spectantia ad dominum.

The term "procurator" was not limited to one named by the bishop to replace or assist him. Thus Innocent III, in a decree suspending the bishop of Langres in 1198, ordered the papal legates to choose a procurator to take his place, one who would now be called an administrator.[9] The same pontiff, in the year 1200, named a subdeacon "procurator tam in spiritualibus quam in temporalibus" of the church of Capua, when a disputed election delayed the choice of a successor to the deceased archbishop.[10] Again, Honorius III informed two archdeacons (who exercised jurisdiction) that they could make a pilgrimage to the Holy Land on condition that they appointed procurators to replace them during their absence.[11] Judicial power, as well, was exercised by a procurator.[12] In an earlier citation it was shown that by the term "procurator" Pope Urban II understood any administrator of ecclesiastical affairs.[13]

The "oeconomus" whom the cathedral chapter was ordered by the Council of Trent to appoint to administer the temporal affairs of a vacant see [14] has, even in recent times, been called a "procurator." Thus Smith:

> Besides choosing a vicar-capitular for the exercise of the *jurisdictio ordinaria episcopalis* — i.e., for the administration proper—the chapter is bound to appoint one or more procurators *(oeconomus),* whose duty it is to take care of the property and revenues of the vacant diocese. In the United States no such procurators or administrators of the temporalities of vacant dioceses are appointed. Vacant sees are usually governed,

---

[9] *MPL,* CCXIV, 506.

[10] C. 19, X, *de electione et potestate electi,* I, 6; Potthast, n. 949.

[11] C. 11, X, *de voto et redemptione voti,* III, 34.

[12] "Sententiam quam venerabilis frater noster R., archiepiscopus vester, per se vel per procuratorem suum tulerit, nos ratam habebimus."—Innocent III, a. 1199—*MPL,* CCXIV, 714. Cf. *supra,* p. 10, the quotation from c. 32, X, *de officio et potestate iudicis delegati,* I, 29.

[13] *Supra,* p. viii; c. 8, C. I, Q. 3.

[14] *Canones et Decreta Concilii Tridentini* (Taurini, 1913), Sess. XXIV, *de ref.,* c. 16. This prescription is repeated in canon 432, § 1.

with us, both in *temporalibus* and *spiritualibus* by one and the same administrator.[15]

The Council of Chalcedon (451) demanded that every diocese have an econome to administer its temporal affairs in dependence on the bishop.[16] The II Plenary Council of Baltimore (1866), referring to this canon of the Council of Chalcedon, urged that every bishop appoint an

> Oeconomum, seu in temporalibus rebus gerendis Procuratorem ... cuius foret muneris domus Episcopalis curam in temporalibus habere, necnon et ecclesiarum bonorumque ecclesiasticorum ad nutum Episcopi temporalem gerere administrationem."[17]

Now it will be seen why the two questions posed at the beginning of this chapter are to be answered together.

1. The reason that the subject of extra-judicial procurators is not as extensively treated in later as in earlier legislation is that many of the functions of the procurator are now exercised by individuals occupying ecclesiastical offices, or at least bearing titles designating their particular capacities, and are treated as such in the Code of Canon Law. Thus:

the term "procurator generalis episcopi" and "vicarius generalis" were practically synonomous; indeed, are made so in the *casus* referred to above;[18]

the term "procurator" was at one time used to designate officials who are now known by more specific titles; such as, administrators, economes, etc.

In the Code one who is named to exercise jurisdiction while not occupying the office to which the jurisdiction pertains, is said to be delegated.[19] Whereas formerly, then, such a one might have been called by the general term of procurator, today he is

---

[15] *Elements of Ecclesiastical Law,* Vol. I, *Ecclesiastical Persons* (9. ed., New York, 1887), p. 421.

[16] Can. 26—Mansi, VII, 400.

[17] *Concilii Plenarii Baltimorensis II Acta et Decreta* (ed. altera mendis expurgata, Baltimorae, 1894), tit. II, c. V, n. 75.

[18] *Supra,* pp. 17-18.

[19] Can. 197, § 1.

known as a delegate.[20] A legate might well be called a procurator of the Holy See, for he is one appointed by the Roman Pontiff with or without ecclesiastical jurisdiction.[21]

2. The nature of the power formerly exercised by extra-judicial procurators was jurisdictional as well as non-jurisdictional. Because, however, of a more accurate determination of principles in regard to jurisdiction and delegation, the term is now applied in extra-judicial affairs to one acting in the name of another in non-jurisdictional matters exclusively. A procurator has, then, what is called by the Code an "officium ecclesiasticum lato sensu;" that is, a "munus quod in spiritualem finem legitime exercetur."[22]

---

[20] But note that the term "delegate" is not always used precisely in this sense in the Code. Thus it is used of one acting with ordinary power; e. g., in canon 267, § 2: "Qui vero mittuntur cum titulo Delegati Apostolici unam habent ordinariam potestatem de qua in § 1, n. 2" (i. e., "advigilare debent in Ecclesiarum statum et Romanum Pontificem de eodem certiorem reddere") "praeter alias facultates delegatas ipsis a Sancta Sede commissas." Observes Maroto: "Nonnulli profecto ex . . . Legatis Papae dicuntur Delegati Apostolici, sed nomini non est insistendum, quoniam et ipsis competit auctoritas ordinaria."—*Institutiones Iuris Canonici ad Normam Novi Codicis* (2 voll., Matriti, 1919), I, 838, *nota* (1).

Again, it is used of one not exercising jurisdiction; e. g., in canon 1094.

[21] Can. 265.

[22] Can. 145. "Procurator est qui aliena negotia de mandato domini administrat. Ex hac notione patet valde differre munus procuratoris a munere delegati; hic enim potestatem publicam seu iurisdictionem exercet, ille potestate mere privata ex contractu mandati acceptata res domini administrat."—Coronata, *Instiutiones Iuris Canonici* (5 voll., Taurini: Ex Officina Libraria Marietti, 1928-1936), I, 328.

PART TWO

THE USE OF EXTRA-JUDICIAL PROCURATORS

INTRODUCTION

The principles governing the use of extra-judicial procurators so far indicated are general in nature, and hence are to be applied, with the exceptions indicated, to all cases. The very first principle, taken from the *Regulae Juris* of the *Liber Sextus*, is that whatever can be done by one's self can be done through another, although relative to the application of this rule there are placed certain restrictions and there are made certain exceptions which have yet to be considered. The other general principles are equally complete and clear, and hence permit of application without any great difficulty. It will be of interest, however, to consider this application in several cases; namely, in those expressly mentioned in the Code of Canon Law.

Since the general norms were so thoroughly propounded and elucidated in the *Corpus Iuris Canonici*, it is not surprising that there is to be found in the *Corpus* little legislation, or amongst the canonists contemporary with it little discussion, pertaining to their application in many particular cases. This is especially true of those cases in which the use of a procurator offered no extraordinary difficulty nor was of unusual occurrence. On the other hand, for cases in which there may have been some question about the possibility of using a proxy, or wherein the conditions under which he could act were more stringent, one must expect to find legislation and comment in greater detail.

Hence, it is not illogical to conclude that, unless a thing is quite obviously of a nature that precludes the intervention of a procurator, lack of legislation in regard to the use of such an agent in a particular case cannot be interpreted as an indication of the illegality of such a use; on the contrary, it rather indicates his acceptance as a legal instrument, since exceptions are to be proved rather than presumed.

CHAPTER I

PROXIES FOR SPONSORS IN THE SACRAMENTS OF BAPTISM AND CONFIRMATION

Article 1. Valid Use of a Proxy

Because there existed no reason for an exception in their case, sponsors in the sacraments of baptism and confirmation were always considered legitimately to have contracted the obligations of their office through procurators. Although the *Corpus Iuris Canonici* contains no direct reference to the use of another in this capacity, the validity of the employment of a proxy for sponsorship in these two sacraments follows naturally from the application of the *Regulae Iuris* cited above. Indeed, it was on these very *Regulae* that later canonists based themselves in discussing such a practice. The Code, then, although clarifying several related topics, introduces no new legislation in the following canons:

Can. 765—Ut quis sit patrinus [in baptismo], oportet:...

5° Baptizandum in actu baptismi per se vel per procuratorem physice teneat aut tangat vel statim levet seu suscipiat de sacro fonte aut de manibus baptizantis.

Can. 795—Ut quis sit patrinus [in confirmatione], oportet:...

5° Confirmandum in ipso confirmationis actu per se vel per procuratorem physice tangat.

The legality of the use of a procurator, then, is perfectly evident. For the valid fulfillment of this function, and therefore for the validity of the sponsorship itself, the proxy must physically touch the one baptized or confirmed or, in the case of the former, hold or receive or raise him from the baptismal font.

Article 2. Spiritual Relationship

The Council of Trent, in attempting to reduce the number of matrimonial impediments, limited the parties who contracted spiritual relationship through baptism to the person baptized, his parents, the minister of the sacrament and the godparents; through confirmation to the confirmed, his parents, the minister and the sponsors.[1] In the chapter of its decrees dealing with this matter, the Council added:

> Quod si alii, ultra designatos [patrinos] baptizatum tetigerint, cognationem spiritualem nullo pacto contrahant . . . [in confirmatione] omnibus inter alias personas huius spiritualis cognationis impedimentis omnino sublatis.[2]

Because the Council, in speaking of the sponsors, used the words "suscipiant" and "tenentem," Sanchez was of the opinion that one who acted as sponsor through a proxy in either of these sacraments did not contract spiritual relationship.[3] He added, moreover, that the procurator did not contract this relationship, since he had not the intention of acting as sponsor.[4] Admitting that this was but an opinion, although he called it "probabilior," he cited the arguments advanced by those who held that the sponsor, even though acting through another, contracted the relationship:

1) since matrimony itself, which is a sacrament, can be contracted through a procurator, *a fortiori* spiritual relationship, an effect of a sacrament, can be;

2) the sponsor takes on the obligation of seeing to the perseverance in the faith of the one for whom he stands; but this obligation, like any other, can be accepted through a procurator;

3) nowhere in the law is the act of the sponsor in these sacraments excepted from the general rule that whatever is done through another has the same effect as if done by one's self.[5]

That the proxy for a sponsor in baptism did not contract spiritual relationship with the baptized is clear from the instructions issued by the Sacred Congregation of the Council to the Bishop of Pisa in April, 1589, to the effect that no dispensation was necessary for the marriage of two parties, one of whom had

---

[1] The Code of Canon Law, in canons 768 and 797, reduced the number of those contracting such a relationship with the one baptized to the minister and the sponsor; with the confirmed to the sponsor only.

[2] Sess. XXIV, *de ref. matrim.*, c. 2.

[3] *De Sancto Matrimonii Sacramento*, lib. VII, disp. LIX, n. 4.

[4] *Ibid.*, n. 10.

[5] *Ibid.*, n. 2.

been proxy for the other's sponsor in baptism.[6] The same principle was enunciated by this Sacred Congregation in the matter of sponsorship in confirmation, when it was declared that a sponsor and not the proxy contracted spiritual relationship with the one confirmed.[7] Even before the Code, then, the sponsor and not his proxy, contracted spiritual relationship with the baptized or confirmed party.[8]

Although accepting the declarations of the Sacred Congregation, Engel (ca. 1634-1674) still maintained that, apart from these declarations, the thesis that neither the principal nor the procurator in such cases contracted the relationship could be defended. He evidently looked upon this relationship as a physical effect rather than the juridical effect that it is; for he insisted that such a defence could show that the procurator contracted no relationship inasmuch as he was not the sponsor; nor did the sponsor, for he had not touched the child; but physical contact during reception of the sacrament was necessary for such a relationship to be contracted.[9]

An interesting case involving a proxy for a sponsor in confirmation was decided by the Sacred Congregation of the Council on June 11, 1881. One Nicholas was asked by Anna to be sponsor for her son. Unable to attend, Nicholas asked Hippolyte to act as his proxy. After the death of her husband, Anna married Nicholas. Some time later, Nicholas asked the diocesan court of Nocera for a declaration of nullity of the marriage on the

---

[6] *Codicis Iuris Canonici Fontes, cura Emi. Petri Card. Gasparri editi* (9 voll., Romae [postea Civitate Vaticana]: Typis Polyglottis Vaticanis, 1923-1939. Voll. VII-IX, ed. cura et studio Emi. Iustiniani Card. Serédi), n. 2206. This collection of volumes will hereinafter be referred to as *Fontes.* Similar decisions were made by the same Congregation on April 19, 1605, and September 13, 1721—*Fontes,* nn. 2355, 3231.

[7] *Nullius,* 15 mart. 1631—*Fontes,* n. 2529; *Collectio Omnium Conclusionum et Resolutionum quae in causis propositis apud Sacram Congregationem Cardinalium S. Concilii Tridentini Interpretum prodierunt ab anno 1564 ad annum 1860, cura et studio Salvatoris Pallottini* (18 voll., Romae, 1868-1895), XII, 579, sub. v. "matrimonium," art. VIII, n. 59. This collection will hereinafter be designated by the compiler's name. Cf. Barbosa, *De Officio et Potestate Episcopi* (Lugduni, 1666), Allegatio XXX, n. 50.

[8] Cf. Reiffenstuel, lib. IV, tit. XI, n. 23.

[9] *Collegium Iuris Canonici* (Beneventi, 1760), lib. IV, tit. XI, n. 6.

grounds that the impediment of spiritual relationship existed between the two parties at the time that the marriage was entered into and no dispensation from it had been obtained. The court issued the decree of nullity. The *defensor vinculi,* basing himself on the words of the Council of Trent, "inter parentes confirmati et tenentem," appealed the case to the Congregation. The decision of the lower court was sustained.[10]

In canons 765, 5°, and 795, 5°, the Code simplifies matters through a fiction of law whereby the sponsor himself is said physically to touch, hold or receive "per procuratorem" the recipient of the sacrament. Hence no spiritual relationship arises between the proxy and the one baptized or confirmed. As Cappello succinctly states: "Qui munus patrini per procuratorem exercet ipse, non procurator, cognationem contrahit." [11]

Article 3. Appointment of the Proxy

A proxy cannot be validly appointed by a third party (for example, the minister or the parents of the one to be baptized) without the knowledge and consent of the principal whom he represents, even though the appointment is afterwards ratified by the principal. This was first stated in a response of the Holy Office, issued on September 15, 1869.[12]

Although the contrary custom was recognized by the Sacred Congregation of the Sacraments, in a response to the bishop of Utrecht, as long as the sponsor knew of the custom and intended to conform to it, nevertheless the custom was reprobated.[13] The same Congregation, upon the issuance of this response, took occasion to append to it an instruction on the importance of the office and duties of sponsors in baptism and confirmation, and to

---

[10] *Thesaurus Resolutionum Sacrae Congregationis Concilii,* CXL (1881), 409. The fact that the mandate was given to the proxy orally was held not to render it invalid.

[11] *De Sacramentis,* I, n. 137. It is well to note that by the law of the Code such relationship constitutes a diriment impediment to marriage only in the case of baptism (can. 1079), although a relationship arises from the act of sponsorship in confirmation (can. 797).

[12] Instr. (ad Administr. Ap. Perthen.)—*Fontes,* n. 1011.

[13] S. C. de Sacramentis, *Ultraiectensis,* 24 iul. 1925—*ASS* XVIII (1926), 43-44.

deplore the disregard for the office and the consequent negligence in executing their duties shown by some sponsors. The salient points of the instruction relative to the matter at hand may be summarized as follows:

1) the intention of the sponsor to accept his obligation through a procurator must be known to the pastor or proved by witnesses or a written document;

2) the name of the procurator as well as the principal must be entered in the baptismal record;

3) the custom of presuming a mandate and of appointing a proxy without the knowledge and consent of the principal is again reprobated;

4) all that is said about the sponsors in baptism applies as well to sponsors in confirmation.[14]

That the consent of the sponsor must be had in the appointment of a procurator is implicitly contained in canons 765, 1°, and 795, 1°, prescribing that for the validity of sponsorship the sponsor must have the intention of performing this function. But he cannot be said to have such an intention if he is entirely unaware that another is accepting the obligation of sponsor for him. Consequently, the custom of presuming a mandate is contrary not only to this instruction of the Sacred Congregation of the Sacraments but to the law of the Code. The practise of presuming the mandate, as is the case with all customs contrary to ecclesiastical laws not expressly forbidding them, becomes valid after continuing for forty years uninterruptedly.[15] Reason demands that even in such a case the conditions for validity stated by this Sacred Congregation be fulfilled; that is, that the sponsor know of the custom and intend—at least in a general way—to conform to it, for no one can have such an obligation imposed on him if he is entirely unwilling to accept it.

---

[14] S. C. de Sacramentis, *Instructio*, 25 nov. 1925—*AAS*, XVIII (1926), 44-47.

[15] "... consuetudo ... neque iuri ecclesiastico praeiudicium affert, nisi fuerit rationabilis et legitime per annos quadraginta continuos et completos praescripta ..."—Can. 27, § 1.

Article 4. Religion of the Proxy

In an instruction of the Holy Office to the Archbishop of Corfu on January 3, 1871, Catholics were forbidden to act as proxies for non-Catholics.[16] Non-Catholics are incapable of validly acting as sponsors,[17] and the intervention of a procurator in no way lessens the invalidating effect of this law. Catholics, on the other hand, are forbidden to be sponsors, even by proxy, for one baptized in an heretical sect.[18] Non-Catholic proxies could validly, but not licitly, act for Catholic sponsors, as has been shown in the treatise on the qualities required of procurators in general.[19]

Article 5. Practical Conclusions

1. It is not necessary that a proxy meet the other requirements, whether for validity or licitness, of a sponsor in these sacraments. Thus one of the parents or a spouse could validly and licitly act as proxy for a sponsor in baptism, although such may not themselves be sponsors.[20] The same parties, as well as one not yet confirmed, could so act in confirmation, despite the fact that they are excluded from sponsorship itself.[21] Although the maximum number of sponsors is one of each sex,[22] the question of sex is immaterial in the choice of a proxy. No particular age is required other than that which is necessary for the execution of such a duty.[23]

2. A rather unusual reason for employing a procurator is found in a reply given by the Congregation of Rites to the bishop of Policastro, Italy. The prelate had asked if, while conferring the sacrament of confirmation, he might at the same time, act as sponsor by signing the forehead of the candidate with the right hand

---

16 "In collatione sacramentorum baptismi et confirmationis haeretici vel schismatici neque per se neque per Catholicum procuratorem . . . patrini munere fungi licite possunt." — *Fontes,* n. 1013.

17 Cans. 765, 1°, 2°; 795, 1°, 2°.

18 S. C. S. Off., instr. (Smyrnen.), 10 maii 1770 — *Fontes,* n. 828.

19 Cf. *supra,* p. 7.

20 Can. 765, 3°.

21 Can. 795, 1°, 3°.

22 Can. 764.

23 Cf. *supra,* p. 4.

and placing the left on his shoulder. The Congregation replied that instead he should serve as sponsor through a procurator.[24] This could be a very practical case for a missionary conferring the sacrament in a particular territory for the first time, and consequently unable to obtain as sponsor one who had already been confirmed.[25]

3. A case in which the use of a proxy in the sacrament of confirmation would make possible the observing of the spirit of the Church's law as well as its letter is that in which the great number of those to be confirmed as compared with the size of the church precludes the possibility of having sponsors present for each individual. The practice, rather common today, of having two members of a parish as sponsors for the whole group being confirmed renders impossible the fulfilling of the obligation imposed on the sponsors, that of seeing to the Christian education of the confirmed,[26] for in many cases the confirmed is entirely unknown to and may never again be seen by the sponsor. If, on the other hand, the same two individuals were appointed proxies for all the sponsors, each *confirmandus* having his own sponsor, not only would the required ceremony have been carried out, but the spiritual relationship established would have some significance and the obligation incurred become capable of fulfillment. Care must be exercised, of course, in seeing that the instructions of the Sacred Congregation of the Sacraments pertinent to this matter are observed.[27] This

[24] S. R. C., *Policastren.*, 14 iun. 1873, ad III — *Fontes*, n. 6059; *Decreta Authentica Congregationis Sacrorum Rituum ex actis eiusdem collecta eiusque auctoritate promulgata sub auspiciis SS. D. N. Leonis Papae XIII* (5 voll. et appendix, Romae, 1898-1912), III, 36, decr. n. 3305.

[25] This is not the only way, however, in which such a difficulty may be solved, as the Sacred Congregation for the Propagation of the Faith indicated in an instruction issued on May 4, 1774: "Verum quia contingere potest, ut in locis missionum nullus adsit, qui antea confirmatus fuerit, permittitur in hoc casu, ut aliqui sine patrino confirmentur, qui postea patrini ceterorum esse poterunt." S. C. de Prop. Fide, instr. 4 maii 1774 — *Collectanea S. Congregationis De Propaganda Fide* (2 voll., Romae, 1907), I, 310.

[26] Can. 797. Moreover, canon 794, § 1, states: "Patrinus unum tantum confirmandum aut duos praesentet, nisi aliud iusta de causa ministro videatur."

[27] S. C. de Sacramentis, *Instructio*, 25 nov. 1925 — *AAS*, XVIII (1926), 44-47. Cf. *supra*, pp. 25-26.

could be done by having the individual sponsors of each of the candidates for confirmation inform the pastor, either directly or indirectly, of their intention to assume this office and request that a proxy be appointed for them to appear at the ceremony. The pastor could then appoint two persons to act as proxies for all the sponsors, thus observing the spirit as well as the letter of the law, and at the same time answering the very practical problem of the limitation of space created by the smallness of the church and the large number of those to be confirmed.

It will be noted that such a practice is not contrary to the above-cited instructions of the Sacred Congregation of the Sacraments, for what was condemned was the custom of presuming the consent of the sponsor, not the practice of permitting another to name the proxy.

CHAPTER II

PROXIES FOR THE CONTRACTING PARTIES IN THE SACRAMENT OF MATRIMONY

The most important instance for employing a procurator in connection with the reception of a sacrament is in the contracting of marriage. In the case of baptism and of confirmation the validity of the proxy's mandate and the manner in which it is carried out have no effect on the validity of the sacraments conferred. But in the contracting of marriage it is otherwise; for here, on the validity of the mandate and on the exactness of its execution depends the validity of the matrimonial contract.

Moreover, the matter itself is of concern not only to the parties but to society itself, a vital social institution being involved. Consequently in marriage by proxy many restrictions are made to the application of the general principles of procuration, and much more detailed legislation is enacted. From the abundance of both past and present legislation as also from the resultant commentary of canonists on the subject, it cannot be concluded necessarily, then, that procurators were or are used more frequently in the celebration of matrimony than in other matters, but rather that there is a greater need of care and clarification in regulating their use in the contracting of marriage.[1]

Article 1. Validity of the Use of a Proxy

The possibility of using a proxy in forming the matrimonial bond follows logically from the contractual nature of this sacrament.[2] Just as other contracts can be made through an agent, so can that which God instituted for the fostering of family life, allowance being made, of course, for any positive law to the con-

---

[1] Cf. *supra*, p. 21.

[2] Cf. Esmein, *Le Mariage en Droit Canonique* (2. ed., par R. Génestal et J. Dauvillier, 2 vols., Paris: Libraire du Recueil Sirey, 1929-1935), I, 189; glossa of c. 8, C. XXX, q. 5, ad v. "uxor."

trary.[3] By its nature, then, marriage is not to be excluded from the class of things to which can be applied the axiom: "Potest quis per alium quod potest facere per seipsum." Of course, reason demands that a proxy be resorted to only when some unusual circumstance prevents the use of the ordinary manner of contracting marriage.[4]

Since its origin is natural, the use of a procurator cannot be said to stem solely from Roman law, as Schiappoli aptly observes,[5] although it is true that in Roman law marriage by proxy was possible.[6] Indeed, this seems but a short step from the contracting of engagements *(sponsalia)* by proxy; and this was a daily practice under the Roman law.[7] But because of the natural origin of this form of marriage and because of the great difference in

---

[3] "Absolute loquendo consensus matrimonialis quavis ratione exprimi potest, sicut consensus in quolibet alio contractu." — Gasparri, *Tractatus Canonicus De Matrimonio* (editio nova ad mentem Codicis I. C., 2 voll., Typis Polyglottis Vaticanis, 1932), II, n. 864. Further references in this work to Cardinal Gasparri's treatise on matrimony will be to this edition unless otherwise indicated.

[4] "Validum est eiusmodi [per procuratorem] matrimonium, etsi raro sit permittendum quibusdam cautelis adhibitis ad rei licentiam." — S. C. C., *Oveten.*, 22 iun., 1894 — *ASS*, XXVIII (1895-1896), 336. Canon 1091 requires that a just cause be present before a pastor may assist at a proxy marriage.

[5] "Il matrimonio per procura del diritto canonico non deriva da quello del diritto romano, ma della teoria che il matrimonio è un contratto consensuale; data l'ugualglianza tra l'uomo e la donna, anche questa si poteva far rappresentare per mezzo di un procuratore." — *Il Matrimonio Secondo Il Diritto Canonico E La Legislazione Concordataria Italiana* (Napoli: L. Alvano, 1932), p. 119.

[6] D. (23.2) 5, 6, 34; *Pauli Libri Quinque Sententiarum,* II, 19, 8, in *Collectio Librorum Iuris Ante-Iustiniani* (3 voll. in 2, ed. Krueger, Mommsen, Studemund, Berolini, 1878), II, 70.

If reference is sometimes made to marriage "per nuntium," it must be remembered that "in iure romano vocabatur nuntius potius quam procurator quia romani conceptum procurationis nimis restringebant, illum extendendo solum ad negotia administrativa, commercialia et iudicialia. Tamen si inspiciatur penitius natura officii illius nuntii ad matrimonium contrahendum similis est procuratori nostro, qui nomine alterius et pro eo init matrimonium, quo aeque accidebat apud romanos." — Kieda, *De Matrimonii Celebratione Per Procuratorem* (Romae: Typis Pontificiae Universitatis Gregorianae, 1939), p. 11.

[7] D. (23.1) 4.

the concepts of the nature of marriage in pagan and in Christian Rome, not too much weight should be placed on an illation from Roman to canon law.

Although the first direct references to proxy marriage in canon law are found in the *Liber Sextus,* these references and the glosses of earlier portions of the *Corpus Iuris Canonici,* as well as the testimony of earlier canonists and historians, indicate that it was an established practice long before the time of the *Liber Sextus.*

Two chapters in the *Decretum Gratiani* dealing with the marriage of Isaac and Rebecca, as related in the twenty-fourth chapter of the Book of Genesis, were made by later glossators and commentators the basis of proof of the legitimacy of proxy marriage; but their true purpose was rather to describe the dispositions becoming a bride.[8] Abraham had sent his servant to Mesopotamia to find a wife for his son, Isaac. The servant encountered Rebecca and, upon obtaining her consent, brought her home to be the wife of his master's son. Ioannes Teutonicus (†1245) commented that Rebecca became the wife of Isaac as soon as she consented to return with the servant and added that this was an argument that matrimony could be contracted between parties who had never seen each other.[9] The strength of the argument is not under discussion at present. What is evident is that in the time of Ioannes Teutonicus the validity of marriage by proxy was taken for granted. He is here concerned with the case in which the parties had never seen each other.

Innocent III (1198-1216), in a response to the Archbishop of Lyons, declared that a woman who had formally taken the veil of widowhood, after going through the marriage ceremony with a certain noble, "mediantibus internuntiis," was held to the marriage bond and was obliged to return to her second husband, unless she had joined a religious order.[10] Again it must be pointed out that in this answer the possibility of marriage being contracted in suchwise was taken for granted; the question and response were concerned rather with a matter relative to the effects

[8] C. 8, C. XXX, q. 5; c. 13, C. XXXII, q. 2.

[9] "Est argumentum quod matrimonium potest contrahi inter absentes qui numquam se viderunt." — *Glossa* of c. 8, C. XXX, q. 5, ad v. "uxor."

[10] C. 14, X, *de conversione coniugatorum,* III, 32.

of marriage. Hence it must be concluded that marriage by proxy was an accepted practice in the time of Innocent III, *a fortiori* in the time of Gregory IX (1227-1241), in whose Decretals (1234) the response is included.

It is not surprising, then, to find the commentators of this period assuming that this sacrament could be received by means of a third party. Vincentius († ca. 1240), in his gloss on investiture in a benefice by proxy, showed that this was valid in view of its analogy to marriage contracted in the same manner.[11] Hostiensis (†1271) not only placed this manner on an equality with the ordinary form as regards the effects but also placed the woman on an equal footing with the man. He concluded the legitimacy of the practice of marriage by proxy from the consensual nature of matrimony for "solus consensus sine traditione facit matrimonium."[12]

---

[11] C. 24, X, *de praebendis et dignitatibus,* III, 5, *glossa ordinaria* ad v. "vel alius," where the gloss of Vincentius is incorporated by Bernard of Parma (†1266).

[12] *Summa,* lib. IV, tit. I, *de sponsalibus et matrimoniis,* pars II, *de matrimoniis,* nn. 7-10. Proceeding from this principle, he was quite logical in denying the necessity of a *deductio in domum* for the validity of marriage, which is sometimes asserted to have been necessary under Roman law. That the *deductio* was necessary in any marriages under this discipline is questionable. Clearly it was not required for certain classes, as C. (5.4) 21 shows. The very principle: "Consensus facit nuptias," is taken from D. (50.17) 30.

"Under the marriage law of the *ius gentium* the mutual consent of the parties took the place of the old time ceremonies. 'Consensus facit nuptias,' said the jurists, although it was contended by some authorities that *traditio,* or delivery of the possession of the wife to the husband, was a necessary element of marriage. The delivery was understood to be made by the conduction of the wife to the home of the husband. It was accordingly held that a man by mere message delivered by another could enter into marriage, provided that the woman was taken to his house. His presence was not necessary. A woman could not, however, by her letter or message be married unless she was afterwards taken as wife to the abode of her husband. The leading of the woman to the house of the man was regarded as evidence of the present intent of the parties, an essential to the bond of marriage, since a consent to be husband and wife at the time the consent is given is quite a different thing from a consent to marry in the future." — Burdick, *The Principles of Roman Law and Their Relation to Modern Law* (Rochester, N. Y.: The Lawyers' Cooperative Publishing Co., 1938), pp. 225-226.

The *Liber Sextus* contains one chapter that is so pertinent to this matter that it may well be quoted in full:

> Procurator non aliter censetur idoneus ad matrimonium contrahendum, quam si ad hoc mandatum habuerit speciale. Et quamvis alias is, qui constituitur ad negotia procurator, alium dare possit: in hoc tamen casu (propter magnum quod ex facto tam arduo posset periculum imminere) non poterit deputare alium, nisi hoc eidem specialiter fit commissum. Sane si procurator, antequam contraxerit, a domino fuerit revocatus, contractum postmodum matrimonium ab eodem (licet tam ipse quam ea, cum qua contraxerit, revocationem huiusmodi penitus ignorarent) nullius momenti exsistit, cum illius consensus defecerit, sine quo firmitatem habere nequivit.[13]

At the risk of repetition to the point of annoyance it must be indicated that this chapter does not institute marriage by proxy. On the contrary, it presupposes its legal standing and decrees what exceptions must be implicitly, if not explicitly, contained in a mandate by which a procurator contracts marriage for another. All of these exceptions have been treated in the discussion of the provisions of the mandate, but they are listed here together:

1) a special mandate was required;

2) the procurator could not substitute another unless that was expressly permitted him;

3) the act of the procurator was null if it was performed after his mandate had been revoked, even though neither he nor the other party had been informed of the revocation.

These provisions will be referred to again in the commentary on the law of the Code which follows.

There is record of a number of historic marriages by proxy during this period. In 1235 Emperor Frederick II (1220-1250) sent envoys to London to contract marriage for him with Isabella, sister of King Henry III of England (1216-1272). On February 22 of that year, in the presence of many witnesses, the envoys confirmed the marriage on the soul of the emperor with

---

[13] C. 9, *de procuratoribus,* I, 19, in VI°.

an oath.[14] Peter della Vigna, leader of the legation, placed a ring on her finger and Isabella was hailed by all present as the empress. Matthew of Paris († ca. 1259) speaks of the new empress being escorted to the emperor at Worms by Henry von Molenarchen, the Archbishop of Cologne, and Henry, Duke of Louvain, "qui, imperatricem ad ipsum honorifice perducentes, matrimonium iam initiatum et ratum procurarent, ut in cognitione carnali fieret consummatum."[15]

In 1516 Vasco Nuñez de Balboa, discoverer of the Pacific, was united in marriage by means of a procurator to Maria, elder daughter of Don Pedro Arias de Avila, governor of the province of Darien in South America. The marriage ceremony took place in Castile while Balboa was in Darien.[16] Mary Tudor, Queen of England (1553-1558), was married to Philip II of Spain (1556-1598) on March 6, 1554, Count Egmont being proxy for the absent Philip.[17]

When the Council of Trent, in the famous *Tametsi* decree,[18] required as a condition for its validity that marriage be contracted in the presence of the pastor and two witnesses, "viro et muliere

---

[14] Allshorn, *Stupor Mundi: Life and Times of Frederick II* (London, 1912), p. 136.

[15] *Matthaei Parisiensis Chronica Majora* (7 voll., ed. by Henry Richards Luard, London, 1876-1883), III, 319. Cf. Slaughter, *The Amazing Frederick* (New York: Macmillan Co., 1937), p. 159. Some modern historians, e. g., Norgate ("Isabella of England"—*Dictionary of National Biography* [63 vols., New York, 1885-1900], XXIX, 62) and Poole ("Germany in the Reign of Frederick II"—*The Cambridge Medieval History* [8 vols., ed. by J. R. Tanner, C. W. Previté-Orton and Z. N. Brooke, New York: Macmillan Co., 1911-1936], VI. 99) speak of the ceremony that took place in London as merely the formal engagement, and the later ceremony at Worms as the true marriage. The language of Matthew, however, is unmistakable.

[16] Quintana, *La Vida de Vasco Nuñez de Balboa* (ed. by George Griffin Brownell, Boston, 1914), p. 49.

[17] Froude, *History of England from the Fall of Wolsey to the Death of Elizabeth* (6 vols., London, 1860), VI, 194. Cf. Kieda, *De Matrimonii Celebratione per Procuratorem*, p. 13, *nota* (22) for other examples of historic marriages by proxy cited from Ludewig, *De Matrimoniis Principum per Procuratores* (Hallae, 1736), *Appendicula*, p. 38; *infra*, p. 36, for examples cited by Pope Benedict XIV.

[18] Sess. XXIV, *de ref. matrim.*, c. 1.

interrogatis et eorum mutuo consensu intellecto," some authors affirmed that marriage by means of a procurator was rendered invalid.[19] Nevertheless, a consideration of the most common opinion of canonists and of the practice and jurisprudence of the Church shows that little doubt existed that the only changes in proxy marriage induced by this decree were the same as those made in regard to the form of any marriage.[20]

Any objections to the use of a procurator in marriage after the Council of Trent are well answered by Sanchez' argument that the aim of the Council in invalidating clandestine marriages was to establish a means of proof that marriage had taken place. Since proof could be had if the proxy marriage was performed before the pastor and witnesses, this aim was attained in such a marriage.[21] Hence, since the contracting of marriage by means of a procurator was not expressly abrogated by the *Tametsi* decree, it retained its validity even after the Council of Trent. This is also the conclusion of De Luca (1614-1683) who, after recalling that the purpose of the decree was to legislate against clandestine marriages, proceeded from the principle that the purpose of a law was of more importance in its application than the formalities used in its expression.[22] Several cases of proxy marriage after the Council of Trent are cited by Pope Benedict XIV to show the practice of the Church in this regard.[23]

---

[19] Cf. Kieda, *op. cit.*, p. 23.

[20] Cf. Lombardi, "De Matrimonio Per Procuratorem"—*ASS*, XXXVII (1905-1906), 189; Ayrinhac, *Marriage Legislation in the New Code of Canon Law* (revised and enlarged by P. J. Lydon, revised ed., New York: Benziger Bros., 1935), p. 216.

[21] *De Sancto Matrimonii Sacramento*, lib. II, disp. XI, n. 20.

[22] *Theatrum Veritatis et Iustitiae* (16 voll., Coloniae Agrippinae 1706), lib. XIV, *supplemen. de matrimonio*, disc. XVI, n. 21. Cf. Pirhing, lib. IV, tit. I, n. 79; Schmalzgrueber, *Ius Ecclesiasticum Universum* (5 voll. in 12, Romae, 1843-1845), lib. IV, tit. I, n. 249; Wernz, *Ius Decretalium*, IV, n. 45; Gasparri, *De Matrimonio* (2. ed., 2 voll., Parisiis, 1892), II, 834.

[23] "Asserimus . . . communem hanc esse opinionem matrimonia quae per procuratorem fiunt, etiam post Tridentinum concilium valida esse; eademque nostris etiam temporibus celebrari et antehac celebrata fuisse, praesertim inter principes; quomodo Henricus IV, Galliarum rex, Mariam Mediceam duxit; et Hispaniarum regis filia cum Austriae archiduce per procuratorem Ferrariae coram Clemente Papa VIII matrimonium inivit."—*De Synodo Dioecesana* (2 voll., Parmae, 1764), lib. XIII, c. XXIII, n. 9.

On June 22, 1894, the Sacred Congregation of the Council refused to declare null a marriage entered into by a girl in the diocese of Oviedo, Spain, and a proxy for a man in Havana, Cuba; but, instead, recommended a dispensation *super matrimonio rato et non consummato.*[24]

Hence the Code is but enunciating the older discipline in canon 1088, § 1: "Ad matrimonium valide contrahendum necesse est ut contrahentes sint praesentes sive per se ipsi sive per procuratorem." It will be noted that this canon asserts the validity of the use of a proxy in marriage, although the following canon, to be commented upon later, contains several provisions affecting the validity of the mandate. Canon 1091 states the requirements for the licit use of a proxy: "Matrimonio per procuratorem... contrahendo parochus ne assistat, nisi adsit iusta causa et de authenticitate mandati... dubitari nullo modo liceat, habita, si tempus suppetat, Ordinarii licentia." To assist at a proxy marriage licitly, then, the pastor must be aware of a reason justifying such action, verify the genuineness of the mandate and obtain the permission of the ordinary, if time permits. Needless to say, failure to fulfill any of these requirements will not affect the validity of the marriage.

Reasons justifying assistance at a proxy marriage would be the desire to regularize a marriage already contracted civilly, to legitimate children already born or to be born, to make possible the legal entry of one party into the other's country, to obtain legal rights (inheritance, insurance, etc.) for the other party, and so forth, when the personal presence of the two parties is impossible or would involve great hardship.

Prior to the Code the permission of the ordinary was not required by universal law, even if time permitted, but was strongly urged by canonists. Scavini (†1881) advised recourse to the ordinary in every case,[25] and a writer in the *Acta Sanctae Sedis* insisted upon the same.[26] This became a matter of particular law in several places. Thus the *Instructio Pro Iudiciis Ecclesiasticis Imperii Austriaci* of May 4, 1855, after acknowledging the validity

[24] S. C. C., *Oveten.*, 22 iun. 1894—*ASS*, XXVIII (1895-1896), 352.

[25] *Theologia Moralis Universa* (3 voll., Mediolani, 1860), III, 576; tract. XI, disp. I, c. 1.

[26] *ASS*, XXVIII (1895-1896), 337.

of proxy marriage, forbade pastors to assist at such marriages without the express permission of the bishop.[27] The I Provincial Council of New Granada, held in 1868, required that the same permission be obtained in writing.[28] The trend toward requiring this added precaution finds its culmination in the universal law of the Code prescribing recourse to the Ordinary in all cases wherein time permits.

Additional provisions may be incorporated in the diocesan statutes.[29] Of such a kind are the prescriptions, including the written acceptance of his duty by the proxy, contained in the instruction issued for marriages of military personnel by the Military Ordinary in the United States.[30]

No regulation existing to the contrary, both parties may be represented by procurators. As to the qualifications of these—their age, sex, religion—what has been said on this subject in general is to be applied here.[31] An *a fortiori* proof for the con-

[27] Tit. I, art. 50—*Analecta Iuris Pontificii* (Romae, 1855-1868; Parisiis, 1869-1891), II (1857), col. 2520.

[28] Tit. IV, c. XI—*Collectio Lacensis* (7 voll., Friburgi Brisgoviae, 1870-1890), VI, 522.

[29] Can. 1089, § 1: "Firmis dioecesanis statutis desuper additis, ut matrimonium per procuratorem valide ineatur . . . "

[30] *Conference Bulletin of the Archdiocese of New York*, XX (1943), 18-29. Hereinafter this *Bulletin* will be referred to as *CBNY*. Cf. the letter of the Sacred Congregation of the Sacraments of May 1, 1932, to the Ordinaries of Italy for special regulations for proxy marriages in that country, particularly for cases in which the groom is resident in the United States.—*Apollinaris*, V (1932), 413-415; also found in Gasparri, *De Matrimonio*, II, 603-605.

[31] *Supra*, pp. 2-7. "Diversitas sexuum in procuratoribus ad contrahendum matrimonium est impertinens; quare duo viri vel duae feminae possunt esse contrahentium procuratores."—Sanchez, *De Sancto Matrimonii Sacramento*, lib. II, disp. XI, n. 15. Cf. Ferraris, *Bibliotheca*, V, 257, sub. v. "Matrimonium," art. I, n. 36; Wernz, *Ius Decretalium*, IV, n. 45; *SRR Dec.*, XX (1928), 370.

"Codex silet de sexu, aetate, religione, etc. procuratoris. Qui proinde, ad valorem quod attinet, potest esse eiusdem sexus ac mandans ipse, cuiuslibet aetatis dummodo procuratorio mandato rite fungi queat, excommunicatus vel interdictus, acatholicus sive baptizatus sive non. Ita iure antiquo, ita quoque, silente Codice, iure novo ad norman can. 6, 3°, 4°. Decet tamen ut catholicus ipse non excommunicatus aliave poena canonica non mulctatus munere procuratoris fungatur."—Cappello, *De Sacramentis*, III, n. 619, 2°.

tention that non-Catholics are prohibited from serving as proxies can be had from the prohibition issued by the Holy Office on August 19, 1891, against the use of non-Catholics as witnesses to a marriage of Catholics;[32] for the procurator plays an even more important role than the witnesses.

In the actual ceremony of marriage the proxy should use his own name but indicate the party for whom he is acting.[33]

Article 2. Sacramental Nature of Proxy Marriage

Melchior Cano (ca. 1509-1560), while forced to admit that marriage contracted through a procurator was valid, could not conceive of a sacrament being conferred on a person who was not physically present for the ceremony by which it was conferred. Hence he concluded that a marriage between two parties, one of whom was absent, was a true marriage, but was not a sacrament, claiming that not only was it not a dogma of faith that every marriage of baptized persons was a sacrament, but that the opposite opinion was more probable.[34]

Cano was but following the opinion of Cajetan (1469-1534), who could see only absurdity in the idea of a person receiving a sacrament while asleep (as might happen in marriage by proxy). The latter author actually seems to have put proxy marriages of baptized persons in the same category as legitimate marriages of the unbaptized as far as effects are concerned, asserting that, since

---

[32] *Fontes,* n. 1144. It will be noted that in the passage quoted in the previous footnote, Cappello says that it is merely becoming that the procurator be a Catholic.

[33] For a complete formula, see *CBNY,* XX (1943), 20; Ayrinhac, *Marriage Legislation in the New Code of Canon Law,* p. 220. Hostiensis (*Summa,* lib. IV, tit. I, *de sponsalibus et matrimoniis,* pars II, *de matrimoniis,* n. 7) gives the essentials of the same formula.

[34] *Opera* (Bassani, 1746), lib. VIII, c. 5. Cano here was logical, but was arguing from the fundamental error that the form of the sacrament of matrimony consisted in the blessing of the priest bestowed on the spouses. Cf. Billot, *De Ecclesiae Sacramentis* (7. ed., 2 voll., Romae: Aedes Universitatis Gregorianae, 1929-1931), II, 362. Cano, a bishop and Dominican theologian, took part in the Council of Trent.

proxy marriage was not a sacrament, it could be more easily dissolved than could a sacramental union.[35]

But the weight of even contemporary theological opinion was against their view that proxy marriage was not a sacrament. Gutierrez (late 16th century) takes a negative argument from the Ecumenical Councils of Florence and Trent to show the sacramental character of such a marriage; for these Councils, in defining the marriage of baptized persons as a sacrament, made no exception in regard to marriage through a procurator.[36] There can no longer be any argument on this point since Pius IX (1846-1878) condemned the proposition that not every marriage between Christians is a sacrament.[37] This teaching is incorporated in canon 1012, § 2. [38]

Article 3. Formalities to be Observed in the Appointment of a Procurator for Marriage

Canon 1089 stipulates several formalities to be observed *ad validitatem* in the issuing of the mandate for a procurator to contract marriage for another:

§ 1—Firmis dioecesanis statutis desuper additis, ut matrimonium per procuratorem valide ineatur, requiritur mandatum speciale ad contrahendum cum certa persona subscriptum a man-

---

[35] *Opuscula Omnia* (Venetiis, 1588), lib. I, tract. XII, q. 1; p. 87. Concina (1687-1756) called this opinion "probabilior." He, too, held the view that the sacrament of matrimony and the marriage contract were separable: "Si Ecclesiae ritus negligant [nupturientes] matrimonium quidem contrahent validum, ratum, perpetuum et indissolubile foedus inducens; secus ut sacramentum." — *Theologia Christiana Dogmatico-Moralis* (10 voll., Romae, 1749-1751), X, 188-189; lib. II, *de matrimonio*, diss. I, n. 25-26.

[36] *Quaestiones Canonicae*, lib. III, c. XLIII, n. 10. Cf. Sanchez, *De Sancto Matrimonii Sacramento*, lib. II, disp. XI, n. 27, 32; Petrus de Ledesma, *De Magno Matrimonii Sacramento* (Venetiis, 1595), quaest. XLII, art. 1, p. 66; Pirhing, lib. IV, tit. I, n. 80; Ferraris, *Bibliotheca*, V, 253-261, sub. v. "Matrimonium," art. I, n. 34-83; *Collegii Salmanticensis Theologia Moralis* (4 voll., Venetiis, 1714), lib. I, tract. IX, c. III, n. 8.

[37] Syllabus Errorum, a. 1864, n. 73 — *Fontes*, n. 543; Pius IX, allocut. *"Acerbissimum,"* 27 sept. 1852 — *Fontes*, n. 515.

[38] "Christus Dominus ad sacramenti dignitatem evexit ipsum contractum matrimonialem inter baptizatos. Quare inter baptizatos nequit matrimonialis contractus validus consistere, quin sit eo ipso sacramentum."

dante et vel a parocho aut Ordinario loci in quo mandatum fit, vel a sacerdote ab alterutro delegato, vel a duobus saltem testibus.

§ 2—Si mandans scribere nesciat, id in ipso mandato adnotetur et alius testis addatur qui scripturam ipse quoque subsignet; secus mandatum irritum est.

The requirement of a special mandate, as has been seen, [39] was contained in the decretal of Boniface VIII on proxy marriage.[40] The provision that the mandate be to contract marriage with a designated person is not of recent origin. Ioannes Andreae (1270-1348), in the gloss of the *Regulae Juris,* remarked that a mandate to marry any good woman is not sufficient; there is required that the particular party be designated.[41] The glossator of Gratian had already pointed out that the parties had to be known to each other in some way; e. g., at least by report.[42]

As for the committing of the mandate to writing, prior to the Code, this was not necessary. De Luca urged that a written document be used in order to observe the purpose of the decree *Tametsi*; that is, to insure the verification of the appointment and, consequently, of the matrimonial contract.[43] A more modern author also advised that the same procedure be followed.[44] But a written document was not required for validity. Thus a fairly recent decision of the Roman Rota on the validity of a proxy marriage which took place before the promulgation of the Code mentions that at that time an oral mandate was valid.[45] The Code, then, is making an innovation in requiring a written document for the validity of the proxy's mandate. This prescription is to be observed even when the principal is unable to write, in which case

---

39 *Supra,* p. 34.

40 C. 9, *de procuratoribus,* I, 19, in VI°. As Pirhing commented: "Nec sufficit mandatum generale in quo expressis quibusdam specialibus, addatur clausula generalis: 'et alia omnia,' quia illa comprehendit solum specialia similia, non autem maiora expressis, ut est causa matrimonii."—Lib. I, tit. XXXVIII, n. 27.

41 *Glossa* of Reg. 68, R. J., in VI°.

42 "In ignotos ex toto consentire non possumus." — *Glossa* of c. 8, C. XXX, q. 5, ad v. "uxor."

43 *Theatrum,* lib. XIV, *supplem. de matrimonio,* dec. XVI, n. 23.

44 Wernz, *Ius Decretalium,* IV, n. 45.

45 *SRR Dec.,* XX (1928), 374; XXIII (1931), 27.

this fact is to be noted in the mandate and an additional witness is required to sign it. It should be remarked that, according to the wording of the canon, if the principal signs the mandate there is need of two witnesses only if neither the pastor nor the Ordinary nor a delegated priest also signs the document.

Article 4. Personal Execution of the Mandate

The oft-quoted chapter of the *Liber Sextus* dealing with marriage *per procuratorem* forbade the deputation of another by the proxy to execute his task, unless this privilege was expressly granted him.[46] The Code retains the prohibition, but without exception, in canon 1089, § 4: "Ut matrimonium validum sit, procurator debet munere suo per se ipse fungi." Woywod is weak in adjudging the force of this latter clause.[47] From the wording of the canon ("debet munere suo per se ipse fungi") and from the fact that a change from the old law is here made with the abrogation of the exception, there can be no doubt that the execution of the mandate by another would render it invalid, even if the procurator had been authorized by the principal to depute another in case of necessity.[48] This does not mean that the principal may not appoint more than one proxy.[49]

Likewise from this paragraph of the canon it is clear that a blank mandate is no longer valid for proxy marriage. In the pre-Code law this was not true, for a blank mandate was interpreted to be the appointment as proxy of the party to whom the mandate was sent, with the faculty to depute another contained implicitly therein.[50] Since such a faculty can no longer be given

[46] C. 9, *de procuratoribus*, I, 19, in VI°.

[47] "The Code demands that the proxy act in person and *seems* to admit no power of subdelegation in the matter."—*A Practical Commentary on the Code of Canon Law* (5. ed. revised, 2 vols., New York: Joseph F. Wagner, 1939), I, 660.

[48] Cf. Cappello, *De Sacramentis*, III, n. 619, 4°; *CBNY*, XX (1943), 18; Kieda, *De Matrimonii Celebratione Per Procuratorem*, pp. 55, 71-74.

[49] Cf. *supra*, p. 12.

[50] Cf. two cases decided by the Sacred Congregation of the Council in which this view was taken of such a mandate: *Neapolitana*, 7 apr. 1883—*ASS*, XVI (1883), 10-27; *Neapolitana*, 14 iun. 1884— *ASS* XVII (1884), 305-313.

even explicitly, a blank mandate is invalid.[51]

ARTICLE 5. CESSATION OF THE MANDATE IN PROXY MARRIAGE

The third section of canon 1089 gives one case in which the mandate ceases, in addition to the general causes of cessation,[52] namely, the insanity of the principal subsequent to the issuance of but prior to the execution of the mandate. Moreover, the same section retains the pre-Code legislation invalidating a mandate immediately upon the revocation and prior to the transmission of this revocation to the proxy or the other party.[53]

A. Insanity of the Principal

Prior to the Code the effect of the insanity of the principal subsequent to the issuance of the mandate but previous to the actual marriage was disputed. At one time, so it appears, the opinion was commonly held that such a marriage was valid.

Sanchez maintained this view, since consent had been manifested and had not been, in fact could not be, revoked.[54] The state of insanity was comparable, as far as its effects on the mandate were concerned, to that of intoxication or sleep, in the opinion of Pirhing, who required that the principal had to be "compos rationis" at the time of issuing the mandate, not necessarily at the time of its execution.[55] Schmalzgrueber, adhering to the same

---

[51] Gasparri, *De Matrimonio,* II, n. 871: "Requiritur mandatum speciale ad contrahendum matrimonium, datum certae ac determinatae personae." Cf. Kieda, *De Matrimonii Celebratione Per Procuratorem,* pp. 87-88. This is not true of all mandates. Riganti *(Commentaria in Regulas, Constitutiones et Ordinationes Cancellariae Apostolicae* [2 voll., Coloniae Allobrogum, 1751], II, 345, Reg. XLV, § 1, nn. 130-131) observes: "De stylo Curiae Romanae passim admittuntur mandata ad resignandum beneficia, relicto in albo nomine procuratoris, qui postea in eo describitur. Et generaliter quod de stylo omnium curiarum tam ecclesiasticarum quam saecularium huiusmodi mandata procurae admittantur."

[52] Cf. *supra,* p. 12.

[53] Can. 1089, § 3: "Si, antequam procurator nomine mandantis contraxerit, hic mandatum revocaverit aut in amentiam inciderit, invalidum est matrimonium, licet sive procurator sive alia pars contrahens haec ignoraverint."

[54] *De Sancto Matrimonii Sacramento,* lib. II, disp. XI, n. 12.

[55] Lib. IV, tit. I, n. 79.

view, denied that subsequent insanity was, in its effect on the mandate, equivalent to death.[56]

On the other hand, Cardinal De Lugo (1583-1660) denied the validity of such a marriage on the grounds that the will of the principal had ceased, unlike the case when he was but asleep.[57] Wernz (1842-1914) resorted to the comparison of subsequent insanity with death[58] and Gasparri (1852-1934), writing prior to the Code, to the claim that as a result of such a state the consent ceased to exist.[59]

It must be admitted that their arguments were not too convincing and hence the matter remained in doubt until the time of the Code. Now there is no doubt of the invalidity of such a mandate and, consequently, of a marriage contracted on the authority of such a mandate. All that would be necessary to prove the nullity of a marriage entered into under such circumstances would be to prove the insanity of the principal at the time of the ceremony. Moreover, as Cappello points out, the canon does not distinguish between perpetual and temporary insanity, and hence is to be applied equally in either case.[60]

B. *Revocation of the Mandate*

That a mandate to marry in the name of another can be revoked is not particularly noteworthy; but that the revocation takes effect immediately, even before the proxy or the other party has been informed, deserves some attention. Upon close consideration this provision, which is not new in the Code but

---

56 "Mors omnia solvit. Ergo etiam consensum ad matrimonium cuius contractum impossibilem reddit; non ita impossibilem eumdem reddit amentia." — Lib. I, tit. XXXVIII, n. 20. For additional support of this side of the question, cf. *Collegii Salmanticensis Theologia Moralis,* lib. I, tract. IX, c. III, n. 105.

57 *Disputationes Scholasticae et Morales* (8 voll., Parisiis, 1869), III, *tractatus de sacramentis in genere,* disp. VIII, n. 108. De Lugo was a contemporary of both Sanchez (1550-1610) and Pirhing (1606-1679). Concina (1687-1756) adhered to De Lugo's opinion—*Theologia Christiana Dogmatico-Moralis,* X, 189; lib. II, *de matrimonio,* diss. I, n. 27.

58 *Ius Decretalium,* IV, n. 45, *nota* (94).

59 *De Matrimonio* (ed. 1892), II, n. 837.

60 *De Sacramentis,* III, n. 619, 3°.

was contained in the *Liber Sextus,* [61] will be seen to be not merely a matter of positive law, but also stemming from the very nature of marriage, since the consent of both parties, freely given, must exist at the time the matrimonial contract is formed.[62]

St. Raymond of Peñafort (†1275), treating of this matter under the aspect of the sacramental rather than the contractual nature of matrimony, gave as the reason on account of which a proxy marriage was not valid if the mandate had been revoked that an *obex* had been placed to the reception of the sacrament; that is, a sacrament could not be validly conferred on one who had formed an intention not to receive it.[63]

The principal difficulty in this connection would be to establish proof that revocation of the mandate was made prior to its execution, as St. Raymond noted in the same passage.[64] This does not mean that the revocation must be expressed, but only that it be demonstrable. Thus an engagement to another,[65] a marriage to another,[66] etc., would imply the revocation of the mandate. One of the reasons on which the Congregation of the Council based

---

[61] C. 9, *de procuratoribus,* I, 19, in VI°. Cf. *supra,* p. 34. Ioannes Teutonicus, in the gloss of c. 8, C. XXX, q. 5, ad v. "uxor," comments: "Requiritur quod duret voluntas prioris, nam requiritur ibi mutuus consensus. Secus tamen est in aliis mandatis, nam licet revocetur mandatum, altero ignorante, tenet tamen contractus."

The Sacred Congregation of the Council declared a marriage null because the mandate had been recalled even though the procurator, unaware of the revocation, had gone through with the marriage ceremony. — S. C. C., *Eugubina seu Perusina,* 25 ian., 5 iul. 1727 — *Fontes,* nn. 3323, 3329.

[62] "In allis contractibus ius potest supplere defectum consensus contrahentium et sine consensu illorum dominium rerum et iura transferre; at vero ad substantiam matrimonii contrahendi requiritur verus et formalis consensus mutuus contrahentium, qui per ius positivum suppleri non potest." — Pirhing, lib. I, tit. XXXVIII, n. 29.

[63] *Summa* (Veronae, 1744), lib. IV, tit. II, *de matrimonio,* § 5.

[64] In the words of Gasparri: "Si mandans, quando procurator matrimonium iniit, consensum etiam mentaliter tantum revocaverat, matrimonium est nullum defectu consensus; sed si revocatio probari nequit matrimonium in foro externo valeret." — *De Matrimonio,* II, n. 874. Cf. Cappello, *De Sacramentis,* III, n. 620.

[65] Coninck (1571-1633), *Commentarium in Universam Doctrinam S. Thomae de Sacramentis et Censuris* (2 voll. in 1, Antverpiae, 1619), disp. 24, dub. IX, nn. 75-76.

[66] Pirhing, lib. I, tit. XXXVIII, n. 29.

its decision in declaring a proxy marriage null was the fact that certain acts of the principal, subsequent to the issuing of the mandate, gave evidence of at least implicit revocation of the mandate.[67]

Article 6. Application of Other Matrimonial Legislation

Other legislation affecting the contracting of marriage in its ordinary juridical form applies equally to marriage by proxy, *servatis servandis.* Thus a marriage in which the principal has issued a mandate to a procurator only "ob vim vel metum gravem ab extrinseco et iniuste incussum" would be clearly invalid.[68] But the acceptance or execution of a mandate would not be rendered invalid by force or fear brought to bear on the procurator, unless the force were irresistible.[69] What is said by the Code relative to the nature and necessity of matrimonial consent, conditions placed on it, knowledge of the purpose and qualities of matrimony and error about the other party[70] pertains to the principal's knowledge, intention and consent, rather than to the procurator's.

If a marriage is contracted by means of a proxy, this should be indicated in the marriage record. Such a procedure was prescribed by the Congregation of the Sacraments in an instruction issued on July 1, 1929, to the bishops and pastors of Italy on the execution of the provisions concerning the celebration of matrimony and its effects as contained in the concordat between the Holy See and the Kingdom of Italy.[71] Although made for a particular territory, this point of the instruction should be followed universally.[72]

Needless to say, from canons 1043 and 1044 the officiant at a proxy marriage receives authority to dispense from impedi-

---

[67] S. C. C., *Neapolitana,* 7 iul. 1736—*Fontes,* n. 3461.

[68] Can. 1087, § 1; S. C. C., *Neapolitana,* 7 iul. 1736—*Fontes,* n. 3461.

[69] Can. 103.

[70] Cans. 1081-1086; 1092-1093.

[71] Art. 35—*AAS,* XXI (1929), 358. The instruction is found in Gasparri, *De Matrimonio,* II, 567-579.

[72] The same prescription is given by the Military Ordinary of the United States for the marriages by proxy of military personnel.—*CBNY,* XX (1943), 29.

ments and the form in the circumstances mentioned in these canons when the proxy has been validly appointed. But an interesting possibility is presented by the following question: may canons 1043 and 1044, insofar as they deal with dispensation from the form of marriage, be applied to canon 1089, § 1, so that the mandate need not be in writing? A case could be imagined in which a priest is asked "ad consulendum conscientiae et legitimationi prolis" to validate the civil union of two parties, one of whom is now in danger of death and unable, due to certain circumstances, to be present for the marriage ceremony either personally or by means of a proxy having a written mandate. Does the power to dispense from the form, granted in canons 1043 and 1044, include the power to dispense from the formalities required for the validity of a mandate for a proxy in marriage? In the opinion of the writer it does.

Although the Code specifically treats of the form of the celebration of matrimony in chapter VI, title VII, book III, not all matters pertaining to the form are treated in this chapter. By the juridic form is meant the sum of those solemnities required by the Church in the manifestation of matrimonial consent.[73] By the positive law of the Church this form consists in the manifestation of consent by the parties, in the presence of each other, personally or through validly appointed procurators [74] before the pastor, the Ordinary or a priest delegated by one of these, and two witnesses.[75] Hence when canon 1094 states that only those marriages are valid which are contracted before the above-mentioned, it is understood that the solemnities required by canon 1088

---

[73] "Solemnitates in matrimonio contrahendo ex iure Ecclesiae adhibendae recte dicuntur matrimonii forma. Pro duplici respectu, qui matrimonio inest, distinguitur forma iuridica, quae directe respicit matrimonium ut contractum, et forma liturgica . . . " — Wernz-Vidal, *Ius Canonicum ad Codicis Normam Exactum*, Vol. V, *Ius Matrimoniale* (Romae: Apud Aedes Universitatis Gregorianae, 1925), n. 524.

[74] Can. 1088, § 1.

[75] Can. 1094.

are observed in the contracting; that is, that the parties or their proxies be in each other's presence.[76]

But when consent is given through another it does not consist solely in the part played by the procurator but also—and, indeed, primarily—in the authorization granted by the principal to the procurator. Hence in proxy marriage the manifestation of consent comprises both the authorization—the giving of the mandate—and the fulfillment of the mandate as morally one action. Now by canon 1089, §§ 1 and 2, this authorization, as has been seen, must be granted in a particular way. Certain formalities are required for the valid authorization of the proxy to act for the principal. But since this authorization is an integral part of the manifestation of consent in proxy marriage, the solemnities attendant upon it constitute part of the form. Therefore the power to dispense from the form of marriage includes the power to dispense from the formalities required in the appointment of a proxy for marriage. Given the circumstances, then, enumerated in canons 1043 and 1044, a dispensation from the formalities of the appointment of a procurator can be granted.

The same line of argument leads to the conclusion that only those bound by the marriage form given in the Code [77] are bound by the formalities required by canon 1089 for proxy marriage. Hence two baptized non-Catholics could contract a valid marriage by proxies who were appointed only orally, or even without proxies though not in the presence of each other, as long as true matrimonial consent is sufficiently manifested.[78] If it is maintained

[76] "Necessaria est amborum contrahentium physica in eodem loco praesentia . . . Contrahentes non sunt, quantum necesse est ad matrimonium valide ineundum, physice praesentes, nisi ita sint in eadem aula, vel in eodem loco, ut alter alterius signa naturali modo percipere possit." — Payen, *De Matrimonio in Missionibus,* Vol. II (Zi-Ka-Wei: Typographia T'oo-Sè-Wè, 1929), p. 118.

". . . necesse est omnino ut contrahentes qua tales, seu dum exprimunt consensum mutuum, sint praesentes ad invicem . . ." — Blat, *Commentarium Textus Codicis Iuris Canonici* (5 voll. in 6, Romae, 1920-1927), III, Pars I, 624.

[77] Can. 1099 lists those who are bound by this form.

[78] "Marriages entered into by letter, provided the contracting parties are not bound by the Catholic form of marriage, are valid."—Petrovits, *The New Church Law of Matrimony* (2. revised ed., Philadelphia: John Joseph McVey, 1926), p. 342.

that canons 1088 and 1089 do not pertain to the form of marriage, then it must be held that they bind baptized non-Catholics, since these are bound by the laws of the Church unless they are explicitly exempted.[79]

Article 7. Proxy Marriage in the United States

The legality of marriage by proxy in the United States depends on the law of the state in which the ceremony is performed. Only one state, Louisiana, forbids such a marriage under the penalty of nullity.[80] There seems little doubt that proxy marriage is legal in those states in which common-law marriages are recognized since, in the words of Lorenzen, English law adopted the provisions of canon law relative to marriage by proxy.[81]

Although several court decisions in the United States, following the *lex loci celebrationis,* recognized the legality of proxy

---

79 Cans. 87, 12, 13, § 1. They are explicitly exempted from the observance of the canonical marriage form by canon 1099.

80 Art. 109, *Louisiana Civil Code,* 1932. But the United States District Court in New Orleans recognized the validity of a proxy marriage celebrated in Constantinople between a woman resident there and a man resident in Louisiana, on the grounds that Turkish law recognized such a marriage. The immigration authorities were ordered to admit the wife to this country.— United States ex rel. v. Tuttle, Dec. 2, 1925 — 12 Fed. (2nd) 927.

81 "Marriage By Proxy And The Conflict of Laws"— *Harvard Law Review* (Cambridge, Mass., 1887 —), XXXII (1918-1919), 481. This entire article (pp. 473-488) is noteworthy for its concise summary of the history and present status of proxy marriage in canon law. Cf. Schouler, *A Treatise on the Law of Marriage, Divorce, Separation and Domestic Relations* (6. ed., edited by Arthur W. Blakemore, 3 vols., Albany, N. Y., 1921), II *(The Law of Marriage and Divorce),* 1458, sec. 1212; Alford, *Jus Civile Matrimoniale in Statibus Foederatis Americae Septentrionalis Cum Jure Canonico Comparatum* (Roma: Anonima Libraria Cattolica Italiana, 1938), pp. 287-288; Kieda, *De Matrimonii Celebratione Per Procuratorem,* pp. 91-93.

The Jurist (Washington, D. C., 1941 —) reports that a bill has been introduced into the Legislature of the State of New Jersey which would permit the contracting of marriage by proxy for the duration of the war, when one of the parties is in the armed forces.—IV (1944), 331.

marriages performed in other countries,[82] the matter is so fraught with the possibility of legal entanglements that marriage by proxy should be resorted to but rarely.[83] However, in two cases such a form of marriage may provide a solution for otherwise insoluble difficulties; namely, in the performance of the *matrimonium conscientiae,*[84] and in the validation of a marriage legally recognized but not celebrated *in facie Ecclesiae.*[85] Of course, the refusal of the civil authority to recognize the marriage of baptized persons in no way affects its validity.[86] Hence when very grave circumstances warrant it, proxy marriage may be resorted to in spite of the risk of failing to obtain civil recognition of the union.

---

[82] Ex parte Suzanna, 295 Fed. 713; Kane v. Johnson, 13 Fed. (2nd) 432; Silva v. Tillinghast, 36 Fed. (2nd) 801; Consulich Società Triestina di Navigazione v. Elting, 66 Fed. (2nd) 534.

[83] "The War Department will not accept a certificate of proxy marriage as the basis for a claim allotment and insurance unless the proxy marriage is recognized as being valid both in the state where it was contracted and in the country where the military subject was stationed at the time of the contract." — *CBNY,* XX (1943), 21.

[84] Cans. 1104-1107.

[85] "It seems that the only proxy marriages which can be arranged with certainty are those which are revalidations of a previous marriage attempted by the two parties before a Protestant minister or a civil marriage. Since the first marriage will have been registered, the civil effects will flow from the same."—*CBNY,* XX (1943), 21.

[86] "Baptizatorum matrimonium regitur iure non solum divino sed etiam canonico, salva competentia civilis potestatis circa mere civiles eiusdem matrimonii effectus." — Can. 1016.

CHAPTER III

PROCURATORS AT COUNCILS

A function of the procurator which has become of less importance in the recent history of the Church is that of substituting for absent prelates at ecumenical, plenary and provincial councils. In canons 224 and 287 for the first time general legislation determines the status of proxies at councils. In the past their status was left undetermined until a question arose concerning it, so that each council had to decide what rôle procurators would play in its deliberations.

ARTICLE 1. ECUMENICAL COUNCILS

In the early days of the Church it was the practice to grant the same status to procurators at ecumenical councils as belonged by right to those whom they represented thereat.[1] Thus Capreolus, Bishop of Carthage, unable to attend the III Ecumenical Council at Ephesus in the year 431, addressed a letter to the Fathers of the Council, informing them that he had delegated Besula, a deacon, to act in his name.[2] In the condemnation of Nestorius the signature of this same Besula is found with those of the bishops present at the Council.[3]

In the V Ecumenical Council (II Constantinople, 553) a number of bishops themselves acted as procurators for others unable to attend.[4] Innocent III, upon summoning the XII Ecumenical Council (IV General Council of the Lateran, 1215) ordered those obliged to attend but unable to do so to send suitable substitutes.[5] In his epistle convoking the XV Ecumenical Council, held at Vienne in 1311-1312, Pope Clement V (1305-1314) named certain archbishops, bishops and prelates from each prov-

[1] "Nam olim ferebant [procuratores absentium] suffragium decisivum non secus ac episcopi a quibus mittebantur et quorum vices gerebant, ut patet ex actis sinodi Nicaenae, Constantinopolitanae I et II, Ephesinae, Chalcedonensis, etc." — Schmalzgrueber, *dissertatio proemalis*, n. 320.

[2] Mansi, IV, 1210.

[3] *Ibid.*, p. 1368.

[4] Mansi, IX, 173-177.

[5] Mansi, XXII, 957.

ince to attend in their own names and to represent those of their provinces not selected, with full power, granted by the absent ones through official documents, to ratify all acts of the Council in their names. Those archbishops and bishops who were not chosen and who were unwilling to carry out this plan were obliged to attend in person or through procurators to whom they were to grant the same authority.[6]

The question of the status of the conciliar procurators was a constant source of irritation in the Council of Trent and a cause of disputes terminated only by the end of the Council. In the bull convoking the Council, Pope Paul III (1534-1549), according to the usual practice, decreed that all those who were obliged to attend but were unable to do so had to be present at least through procurators.[7] So many of the prelates who were obliged to attend the Council took advantage of this privilege[8] that Paul III, on April 17, 1545, decided that proxies for absent members enjoyed no vote in the assembly, but merely had the duty of offering and proving the reason for the absence of their principals.[9]

On December 5 of the same year, however, the pontiff, in a letter to the cardinal legates of the Council, made an exception for the German hierarchy. Because of the inroads on the faith being made in their country and the consequent need of their

6 "Quod si forsan ipsis archiepiscopis et episcopis accessuris huiusmodi noluerint concedere potestatem, eo casu venire vel alios procuratores idoneos cum potestate simili ad idem teneantur concilium destinare."—Mansi, XXV, 374.

7 *"Initio nostri,"* 22 maii 1542—*Canones et Decreta,* p. xiv.

8 Hefele-Leclercq (*Histoire des Conciles* [10 vols in 19, Paris: Libraire Letouzey et Ané, 1907-1938], IX, 1. par., 216) claim that only eighteen archbishops and bishops, excepting the papal legates, were present for the opening of the Council. The same authors (*ibid.,* pp. 210-211) indicate, however, that the fewness of those in attendance was not due exclusively to the indifference of the prelates, but in many cases to interference by the secular power. Thus the King of Naples requested the bishops of his realm to name four of their number to represent all, hoping thus more easily to control the Neapolitan representation at the Council and at the same time retain its numerical strength, for he was under the impression that the four would enjoy the votes of all.

9 *Concilii Tridentini Diariorum, Actorum, Epistularum et Tractatuum Nova Collectio* (13 voll., ed. Societas Goerresiani, Friburgi Brisgoviae: B. Herder, 1901-1938), IV, 405-406.

presence there, they were to be granted the privilege of sending procurators who would have a vote in the conciliar assemblies. Nevertheless, the promulgation of this privilege was left to the discretion of the legates.[10] The legates, fearful lest the announcement of the granting of this privilege to the German bishops would arouse a protest among the other members of the Council,[11] made no public mention of it, although the privilege was not revoked. They did manage to have the Council itself petition the pope to grant the procurator of Otto, Cardinal Archbishop of Augsburg, a consultative vote. The pope granted the request.[12]

More bickering followed, from time to time, over the question of the power of the procurators. In 1546 Dominicus Sotus (1494-1560), the theologian, was refused a vote in the assemblies as proxy for the Master-General of the Dominicans, although he remained as a consultor to the Council.[13]

Once more, on December 29, 1561, a new mandate of the Cardinal Archbishop of Augsburg was read, naming Francisco Piccolomineo, himself a bishop, the cardinal's procurator at the Council. Ercole Gonzaga (1505-1563), Cardinal Archbishop of Mantua and papal legate at the Council, asserted that this was contrary to the prescription of Paul III, but conceded this prelate the privilege he had enjoyed before.[14] Two days later Pius IV (1559-1565), the then ruling pontiff, renewed this prescription of Paul III, mentioning that even if bishops served as procurators for other prelates, they enjoyed only one vote.[15]

On July 20 of the following year, the assembly was thrown into a turmoil when Massarelli (1510-1566), the secretary, accepted the votes of the procurators of the Bishops of Salzburg and Eichstätt on the grounds that the privilege granted the Ger-

[10] *Ibid.*, pp. 443-444.

[11] Pallavicini, *Vera Concilii Tridentini Historia* (3 voll., Antverpiae, 1670), lib. XX, c. XVIII, n. 8. (This work will hereinafter be referred to by the author's name.) The legates expressed this fear in their letter of December 14, 1545, to Cardinal Farnese. — *Conc. Trid. Diariorum, etc.*, X, 277.

[12] Pallavicini, lib. VI, c. II, nn. 6-7.

[13] *Ibid.*, n. 5.

[14] *Conc. Trid. Diariorum, etc.*, VIII, 267-269.

[15] *Ibid.*, pp. 269-271.

man hierarchy by Paul III had never been revoked or expressly abrogated.[16] Finally, on August 26, 1562, Pius IV revoked the privilege that had caused so much dissension,[17] and neither a deliberative nor a consultative vote was given to another procurator during the Council, although both German and French members, up to its very conclusion, argued for greater representation.[18]

The last disposition of the Council concerning procurators was that they, unlike the voting members, should not add the word "definiens" when subscribing to the canons and decrees of the Council.[19]

The contentions at the Council of Trent over the subject of procurators showed those who made preparations for the Council of the Vatican more than three hundred years later the necessity of settling this problem at the outset. In the document announcing the Vatican Council, Pope Pius IX reminded those who were obliged to attend that they were subject to punishment if absent unless, prevented from coming by a just cause, they sent proxies to offer their excuses to the Council.[20]

The historian Hefele (1809-1893), a member of the Central Commission preparing for the Council, argued for the right to vote for the procurators of absent members,[21] asserting that only

---

[16] *Ibid.*, p. 721; Pallavicini, lib. XX, c. XVII, n. 8. The secretary had acted without consulting the legates and was reprimanded by them for his action.—*Conc. Trid. Diariorum, etc.*, I, lxxvii.

[17] *Conc. Trid. Diariorum, etc.*, IX, 36.

[18] Because of the voteless status of the proxies, one German bishop remarked in the assembly of May 17, 1563: "Nescio quomodo concilium hoc generale dici possit."—*Ibid.*, p. 504; Pallavicini, lib. XX, c. XVII, n. 17.

[19] *Conc. Trid. Diariorum, etc.*, IX, 508. The absence of the word may be noted in the same volume, p. 1119. Cf. Pallavicini, lib. XXI, c. I, nn. 9-14; Benedictus XIV, *De Synodo Dioecesana*, lib. XIII, c. II, n. 3. Pallavicini (1606-1667) waxes rhetorical in describing the settlement of the issue: "Ita palam fit, duriora quaedam, quae initio videntur impatibilia instar quorumdam silvestrium pomorum concocta et maturata, tempore ac tractatione paulatim mitescere et absque molestia deglutiri."—*loc. cit.*, n. 14.

[20] Litt. ap. "*Aeterni Patris,*" 29 iun. 1868—*Fontes*, n. 551.

[21] The Commission had decided on June 14, 1868, that proxies would have neither deliberative nor consultative votes.—Mansi, XLIX (curantibus Ludovico Petit et Ioanne Baptista Martin), 501; *Coll. Lac.*, VII, 1061.

if they were granted suffrage would the whole Catholic world be represented in the voting of the Council.[22] The secretary of the Central Commission wrote on August 18, 1869, to the acting Secretary of State that procurators of absent members were entitled to no vote and that their rôle was simply one of proving the legitimacy of their principals' reasons for absence and of conveying to the latter the results of the Council.[23] The Commission had already, however, granted procurators the right to assist at public sessions, but not at general assemblies.[24] The pope then granted them permission to remain at the sessions even during the voting.[25]

Canon 224 retains this same discipline; namely, requiring those who are called to ecumenical councils, but who cannot attend, to send procurators to explain their absence. The procurators as such enjoy neither a deliberative nor a consultative vote and may assist only at public sessions. If one having a right to assist at the council acts as proxy for an absent member, he enjoys only one vote. It is clear from this that the Code permits one accredited member of the council to represent another. No objection can be made to having one procurator act for several absent members.

Article 2. Provincial and Plenary Councils

The alleged IV Council of Carthage, referred to as a provincial council, held in 398, in a decree later included in the *Decretum Gratiani*[26] required all bishops unable to attend the council to send legates to represent them.[27] A perusal of the acts of any of

---

[22] Mansi, XLIX, 533; *Coll. Lac.*, VII, 1088. Bouix (*De Papa et Concilio Oecumenico* [3 voll., Parisiis, 1870], III, 397) had expressed the same hope. A footnote mentions that the hope was in vain.

[23] *Coll. Lac.*, VII, 1062.

[24] January 31, 1869 — Mansi, XLIX, 519-520, 612; *Coll. Lac.*, VII, 1062.

[25] *Coll. Lac.*, *loc. cit.*

[26] C. 9, D. XVIII.

[27] "Episcopus ad sinodum ire non tardet, nisi satis gravi necessitate inhibeatur; sic tamen, ut in persona sua legatum mittat, suscepturus, salva fidei veritate, quidquid sinodus statuerit."—Can. 21; Mansi, III, 953. The word "sinodus" was not confined, as today, to the designation of a diocesan assembly. Cf. Wernz, *Ius Decretalium,* II, n. 858, *nota* (1).

those councils which include a list of the members present will show to how great an extent this practice was followed.

Another canon in Gratian seems to touch directly on the point of representation by proxy at a provincial council, and was thus interpreted by the decretists; but closer inspection reveals that it rather referred to a bishop who had to defend himself in a civil or criminal case before a council.[28]

The sending of a procurator was not merely a right; it was a duty, and consequently absent prelates were obliged to send representatives to councils.[29] Bouix (1808-1870) cites the heavy penalties imposed by the Provincial Council of Bordeaux (1624) on the Bishop of Sarlat because of his failure to send a proxy in his absence from the Council.[30]

The practice of permitting the nature of the proxies' vote to be determined by the *de iure* accredited members of each council resulted from the general application made of a reply of the Sacred Congregation of the Council to the Provincial Council of Trani (1589) to that effect.[31] The Congregation in its reply stated that unless the Council explicitly granted a deliberative vote to the procurators they enjoyed only a consultative one. The Council of Trani did, in fact, grant a deliberative vote to the procurators. The same Congregation repeated these instructions for the I Provincial Council of Westminster (1852), leaving to the Council itself to determine the proxies' status in regard to the voting. The Council permitted the proxies to have only consultative votes.[32] Hence the practice persisted of allowing each council to settle this question for itself.

---

[28] C. 1, C. V, q. 3. Cf. *Capitula Angilramni, apud Decretales Pseudo-Isidorianae et Capitula Angilramni* (ed. Paulus Hinschius, Lipsiae, 1863), pars IV; Rufinus, *Die Summa Decretorum des Magister Rufinus* (ed. Heinrich Singer, Paderborn, 1902), commentary on canon cited.

[29] S. C. C. *Tarentina,* 2 apr. 1595 — Pallottini, XVI, 615.

[30] *De Concilio Provinciali* (2. ed., Parisiis, 1862), p. 125.

[31] Pallottini, XVI, 615. Cf. Barbosa, *Summa Apostolicarum Decisionum* (Lugduni, 1685), p. 8, coll. II, n. 8; Fagnanus, *Commentaria in Quinque Libros Decretalium* (5 voll., Venetiis, 1709), III, 217, n. 54, commentary on c. 10, X, *de his quae fiunt a praelatis sine consensu capituli,* III, 10; Ferraris, *Bibliotheca,* II, 434, sub v. "Concilium," art. II, n. 18; Bouix, *De Concilio Provinciali,* p. 125.

[32] *Coll. Lac.,* III, 897.

In the United States no established policy was followed. At the III Provincial Council of Baltimore (1837) Bishop Dubois of New York was represented by a proxy, Father Felix Varela, vicar general of the diocese, who had only a consultative vote.[33] But at the IX Provincial Council of Baltimore (1858) procurators of absent members enjoyed deliberative votes.[34] On the other hand, the II Provincial Council of New Orleans (1860) granted to the proxy of Bishop Chalon of Mobile only a consultative vote.[35] No doubt this variety of practice left something to be desired. At any rate, the Fathers of the II Plenary Council of Baltimore (1866) ruled that at all their provincial councils the procurators of absent prelates would enjoy deliberative votes.[36]

The freedom to determine the status of proxies attending them seems to have been permitted to plenary councils as well. The members of the I Plenary Council of Australia (1885) at their first private session granted procurators at the Council deliberative votes.[37] In summoning the III Plenary Council of Balti-

[33] It was at the first private congregation that the prelates, after accepting Father Varela's mandate, decided that he would be accorded a consultative vote. — *Concilia Provincialia Baltimori habita ab anno 1829 usque ad annum 1849* (editio altera, Baltimori, 1851), p. 125; *Coll. Lac.*, III, 50.

[34] *Concilium Baltimorense Provinciale IX* (Baltimori, 1858), p. 12; *Coll. Lac.*, III, 171.

[35] *Coll. Lac.*, III, 249. For examples of differences in practice in the ecclesiastical provinces of France, cf. *Coll. Lac.*, VI, 448, 852, 1095.

[36] *Concilii Plenarii Balt. II Acta et Decreta*, tit. II, c. III, n. 60. It is interesting to compare the wording of the commentary on this subject in two editions of Smith's *Elements of Ecclesiastical Law* (vol. I, *Ecclesiastical Persons)*. In his fifth edition (1883) this author asks (p. 36): "What persons, according to the Second Plenary Council of Baltimore, should be present at and therefore called to provincial councils?" And he answers: "These persons . . . procurators or representatives of Bishops lawfully absent . . . All these have, *iure communi*, a decisive voice or vote." But in the ninth edition (1887) the same author writes (p. 37-38): "The following have only a consultative vote, by the general law: . . . procurators of bishops lawfully absent. All these may receive the right of casting a decisive vote, if the council consents. In the United States it is the custom for all of these persons . . . to cast a decisive vote." The later edition states the matter correctly.

[37] *Acta et Decreta Concilii Plenarii Australasiae I* (Sydney, 1887), p. xxii.

more (1884), Cardinal Gibbons reminded the prelate-members of their duty to send procurators in the event that they were prevented from attending.[38] In the preliminary congregation of archbishops and bishops it was agreed to grant deliberative votes to these procurators.[39] This marked a change from the method observed in the II Plenary Council of Baltimore (1866) in which the proxies' right to a deliberative vote was stated explicitly in Archbishop Spalding's letter summoning the Council.[40]

The matter is now very specifically determined for both provincial and plenary councils in canon 287. While reaffirming the obligation of absent members to send procurators, the canon limits these procurators to a consultative vote.[41] A member of a council may serve as proxy for another member, but does not thereby enjoy greater voting power than he already had.

No special qualifications appear to be demanded of such procurators other than that they possess a status recognized as fitting them for the fulfillment of their duty.[42]

---

[38] *Acta et Decreta Concilii Plenarii Baltimorensis Tertii* (Baltimorae, 1886), p. xxi.

[39] *Ibid.*, p. xxv. It will be noted that the procurators signed the decrees of the Council in the same manner as the *de iure* attending members signed, "*definiens subscripsi.*"—*Ibid.*, p. 188.

[40] *Concilii Plenarii Balt. II Acta et Decreta*, p. xiv; *Coll. Lac.*, III, 327. Father Coosmans, the only procurator in attendance, signed the decrees of the Council "*definiens subscripsi.*"—*Concilii Plenarii Balt. II Acta et Decreta*, p. 274; *Coll. Lac.*, III, 546.

[41] On the grounds of a legitimate contrary custom, the IV Provincial Council of Portland in Oregon (1932) granted the procurator of an absent bishop a deliberative vote. The procurator signed the decrees of the Council "*definiens subscripsi.*" A footnote explains: "Votum deliberativum Procuratori Seattlensi haud potuit denegari, cum consuetudo contraria satis diu apud nos vigens, propter peculiaria locorum ac personarum adiuncta, prudenter submoveri non posse videretur."—*Acta et Decreta Concilii Provincialis Portlandensis In Oregon Quarti* (Portlandiae, 1934), p. 138.

The decretum recognitionis was issued by the Sacred Congregation of the Council on February 16, 1934, the form of the procurator's signature remaining unchanged.

[42] " . . . sufficere quod Procuratores sint habiles, Doctores et discreti." S. C. C., *Tarraconen.*, 4 dec. 1638—*Fontes*, n. 2596.

CHAPTER IV

THE USE OF PROCURATORS IN OTHER MATTERS

Article 1. Investiture in a Benefice

Canon 1445 explicitly states that a benefice may be taken possession of through a procurator having a mandate for this act.[1] This is by no means an innovation in canon law, for the same practice was admitted in a response of Innocent III in the year 1200.[2] But in the taking possession of a benefice which must be preceded by a profession of faith,[3] it remains the duty of the beneficiary to make the profession personally.[4] The profession of faith may be received, however, through a delegate,[5] although this was not formerly permitted.[6]

A bishop, in taking possession of his diocese, may employ the services of a procurator to show to the cathedral chapter (or diocesan consultors) the necessary letters from the Holy See.[7]

---

[1] "Possessio beneficii etiam per procuratorem, speciale mandatum habentem, capi potest." Conversely, any ecclesiastical office may be resigned through a procurator.—Can. 186.

[2] "Clericus absens per alium, vel alius magis pro ipso poterit de beneficio ecclesiastico investiri." — C. 24, X, *de praebendis et dignitatibus,* III, 5; Potthast, n. 1066. Cf. also c. 17, *de praebendis et dignitatibus,* III, 4, in VI°.

[3] Can. 1443, § 1: "Nemo possessionem beneficii sibi collati aut propria auctoritate capiat, aut non emissa fidei professione, si agatur de beneficiis pro quibus haec fidei professio praescripta sit."

[4] "Procurator ad possessionem beneficii capiendam emittit, quidem, professionem in actu posessionis sicut alias formulas rituales pronuntiat et symbola; v. g., biretum, anulum, etc., contrectat vel assumit, sed manet instituto vel mandanti, idest beneficiato, onus emittendi professionem fidei ad normam can. 1407."—Pistocchi, *De Re Beneficiali iuxta Canones* (Taurini: Officina Libraria Marietti, 1928), p. 232. Cf. *infra,* pp. 71-72.

[5] Can. 1406, 7°.

[6] "An de iure communi possit Episcopus subdelegare omnes sacerdotes suae dioecesis ut possint dare investituram, seu mittere presbyteros institutos in possessionem beneficii, et professionem orthodoxae fidei audiant? R. Ordinarium quoad immissionem in possessionem posse delegare; quo vero ad fidei professionem excipiendam, non posse." — S. C. Ep. et Reg., *Apamien.,* 14 apr. 1890 — *Fontes,* n. 2016. Cf. Wernz, *Ius Decretalium,* III, n. 18.

[7] Cans. 334, § 3; 427.

ARTICLE 2. THE *Ad Limina* VISIT

Canon 342 states that the visit which a bishop must make to the Holy See every five or ten years, depending on whether he is in or out of Europe,[8] may be made through his coadjutor, if he has one, or, for reasons which have been approved by the Holy See, through a priest who resides in the bishop's diocese. The Constitution *Romanus Pontifex* of Sixtus V (1585-1590), issued on December 20, 1585, stated that the procurator must show proof of the existence of the reason preventing the bishop from satisfying this obligation personally.[9] The present legislation indicates that the reason must be demonstrated to the Holy See before the procurator may be sent.

On several occasions the Holy See refused to permit a priest resident in Rome to serve in this capacity.[10] The same action was taken on a request to permit a priest from his diocese to fulfill a bishop's obligation in this matter, the reason for the refusal being that this was not the particular purpose of the priest's visit to Rome.[11] Benedict XIV, however, attested to the fact that the Holy See, in more recent years, had mitigated its policy and, because of difficulties and expenses in traveling, had permitted a bishop to appoint as his representative in this visit a priest who had gone to Rome for other reasons; moreover, a religious could be chosen for this act, although formerly such was not the case.[12] The Sacred Congregation of the Council quoted the words of Benedict XIV with approval of both these points in its instruction on the subject.[13]

---

[8] Can. 341.

[9] § 4—*Fontes,* n. 156.

[10] S. C. C., *Quiten.,* 16 mar. 1647; *Eistetten.,* 24 febr. 1652—*Fontes,* nn. 2672, 2719.

[11] S. C. C., *Melevit.,* 14 dec. 1652—*Fontes,* n. 2723.

[12] *De Synodo Dioecesana,* lib. XIII, c. VI, n. 3. Sixtus V, in the above-cited constitution *(loc. cit.)* explicitly permitted a religious to be employed in this task if a diocesan priest was not available.

[13] *De Visitatione Sanctorum Liminum Instructio S. C. Concilii,* edita iussu S. M. Benedicti XIII, exposita et illustrata per Angelum Lucidi (3. ed., per Iosephum Schneider, 3 voll., Romae, 1883), c. I, nn. 29-30; c. III, nn. 64-66.

The Sacred Congregation of the Propagation of the Faith, in its instruction of June 1, 1877, also quoted Benedict XIV to this effect and stated that all that was required of the priest so chosen was that he be sufficiently acquainted with the affairs of the Church and of the diocese to be able to fulfill his rôle properly.[14]

A slight difference is to be noted between the language of the Code in canon 342 and that of the decree of the Sacred Consistorial Congregation on the same subject. The former uses the phrase "per idoneum sacerdotem qui in eiusdem Episcopi dioecesi resideat;" the latter, "per idoneum sacerdotem qui in eadem dioecesi stabilem commorationem teneat."[15]

Article 3. Procurators in Religious Institutes

The question discussed by Suarez (1548-1617) concerning the validity of a religious profession made by proxy is of no practical importance, since the Code permits the authorized superior of a religious institute to depute another to accept the profession, thus obviating the necessity of a novice appointing a proxy at any time.[16] The above-named author argued that unless the law contained a prohibitory exception in a particular case, any contract could be entered into through another; and since religious profession was a contract, it could be made by proxy.[17] Although generally referred to as a delegate, one who receives a profession in a religious congregation in the name of the authorized superior is more properly called a procurator, since he is not thereby exercising jurisdiction. The superior may give a general deputation for this act.

Canon 517 requires that every religious institute of men enjoying papal approbation have a General Procurator to the Holy

[14] S. C. de Prop. Fide, instr. 1 iun. 1877, n. 11 — *Collectanea,* II, 108, n. 1472; *Acta et Decreta Concilii Plenarii Balt. III,* p. 200. Cf. Benedictus XIV, *De Synodo Dioecesana,* lib. XIII, c. VI, n. 3.

In its decrees, the III Plenary Council of Baltimore (1884) specifically mentioned that the bishop had to fulfill this duty through a procurator if he could not perform it personally.—Tit. II, c. I, n. 13.

[15] S. C. Consist. decr. 31 dec. 1909, Can. IV, § 3 — *Fontes,* n. 2064.

[16] Can. 572, § 1, 6°.

[17] *Opera Omnia* (26 voll., editio nova a Carlo Berton, Parisiis, 1856-1866), XV, lib. VI, c. XII, n. 22.

See, who is to handle all affairs between the Holy See and the institute and its members. This does not exclude the right, of course, of an individual religious to communicate directly with the Holy See in some extraordinary case.[18]

The name "procurator" is often given also to economes [19] or to other administrative assistants in religious institutes (mission procurator, procurator for a particular work, etc.); and properly so, for these agents are "pro aliis curatores," acting in particular matters for the other members of their institute.

---

[18] Can. 611.
[19] Can. 516.

CHAPTER V

EXCEPTIONS TO THE USE OF A PROCURATOR

There are some cases in which either the nature of the matter or the positive law of the Church prevents the application of the principle that whatever can be done by oneself can be done through another.

Among the things which, by their nature, exclude the use of a procurator are those which are to be done by virtue of the power of orders, of consecration, of jurisdiction if it cannot be delegated and, in general, the things which are to be done by one chosen for such tasks *intuitu personae.* It is not possible, however, to carry this exclusion to the extent to which secular law carries it in regard to agency; namely, to the exclusion of any purely personal act or duty.[1] Pistocchi seems to indicate that a profession of faith cannot be made through another because of its personal nature;[2] but what is more personal than marriage, which can be contracted by proxy, or an oath which, at one time, could be taken through another?

In those sacraments in which the power of orders is necessary in the minister for their valid administration, a mandate cannot

[1] Cf. Mechem, *Outlines of the Law of Agency,* pp. 23-24, sec. 41. But note how closely this author, in the same passage, agrees in principle with what is stated above: "Agency cannot lawfully be created for the performance of an act which from its nature, or the terms of the law requiring it, can only properly be performed by the principal in person." He continues: "The rule in this class of cases is sometimes stated in this way: that authority cannot be delegated for the performance of a purely personal act or duty."

"While it is a maxim of the common law that whatever a person may do of his own right with relation to property he may do by another, yet there are certain exceptions to this general rule, and there are acts of so peculiarly personal a nature that their performance cannot be delegated. To this class of cases belong making of wills, contracting of marriage and especially the discharge of duty which is created by statute, and which, by the express terms or necessary effect of the act, are required to be performed by the person only who is named therein."—Commonwealth v. Farmers' and Shippers' Tobacco Warehouse Co., 52 S. W. 799.

[2] *De Re Beneficiali iuxta Canones,* p. 225. Cf. *infra,* p. 72, for an account of the controversy between earlier canonists as to whether or not the profession of faith could be taken by proxy.

be given to another through which the power itself is exercised.[3] Several examples of this are cited in the *Corpus Iuris Canonici*. Thus in the ordination of a priest the bishop who administers the sacrament may not impose his hands while deputing another to pronounce the form.[4] Sacramental confession must be made personally, not merely by proxy.[5]

Canon 887 requires that the penance imposed by the confessor in sacramental confession be performed by the penitent himself.[6] Pope Alexander VII (1655-1667) condemned the proposition that the penitent could choose a substitute to fulfill this obligation.[7] Indeed, since the penance imposed in confession is by nature vindictive[8] it must be performed by the one guilty of the sin for which it was imposed. Satisfaction being an integral part of the sacrament of penance,[9] the penitent must perform it just as he must supply the other parts, contrition and confession.[10]

---

3 When a priest, in virtue of a special faculty granted him by law or indult, confers the sacrament of confirmation, he does so not as a procurator, but by virtue of the power of orders which is his, but which cannot be validly exercised without such a faculty. Cf. Billot, *De Ecclesiae Sacramentis,* II, 309.

4 C. 14, D. XXIII; *glossa* of Reg. 68, R. J., in VI°.

5 C. 88, D. 1, *de poenit.; glossa* of Reg. 68, R. J., in VI°. The use of an interpreter in confession, as permitted by canon 903, is quite a different matter; for in such a case the penitent confesses his sins and receives absolution personally.

6 "... quas [satisfactiones] poenitens volenti animo excipere atque ipse per se debet implere."

7 S. C. S. Off., decr. 24 sept. 1665, prop. 15, damn.—*Fontes,* n. 734; Denziger-Bannwart-Umberg, *Enchiridion Symbolorum, Definitionum et Declarationum de Rebus Fidei et Morum* (6. et 7. ed., Friburgi Brisgoviae: Herder et Co., 1928), n. 1115.

8 "Habeant [sacerdotes] autem prae oculis, ut satisfactio quam imponunt non sit tantum ad novae vitae custodiam et infirmitatis medicamentum, sed etiam ad praeteritorum peccatorum vindictam, et castigationem."—Conc. Trident., sess. XIV, *de poenitentia,* c. 8.

9 Conc. Trident., sess. XIV, *de poenitentia,* c 3.

10 "Poenitentiam a confessario iniunctam poenitens ipse implere debet: praeceptum enim poenitentiae exigit actionem personalem quae per alium impleri nequit. Et sane actiones, quae ad sacramentum sive essentialiter, sive integretaliter constituendum requiruntur, ab ipso suscipiente peragi debent; sicut ergo contritio et confessio per alium peragi non potest, ita nec satisfactio."—Noldin, *Summa Theologiae Moralis,* Vol. III, *De Sacramentis* (25. ed., recognovit et emendavit A. Schmitt, Oeniponte/Lipsiae: Typis Feliciani Rauch, 1938), p. 312.

The famous canon of the IV Lateran Council (1215) which required every Catholic to receive the sacrament of penance at least once a year, also ordered penitents to fulfill the imposed penance "propriis viribus."[11]

Article 1. The Diocesan Synod

The Code expressly forbids the use of procurators in diocesan synods. Canon 359, § 1, reads: "Iis qui ad Synodum venire debent, si legitimo impedimento detineantur, non licet mittere procuratorem qui eorum nomine Synodo intersit; sed Episcopum de impedimento certiorem faciant." This legislation is not new with the Code; nor is it, strictly considered, entirely positive legislation, for the nature of a synod precludes the necessity of representation, since it is not a law-making body, the bishop being the sole legislator and all others in attendance having only consultative votes.[12]

While it is true that the Sacred Congregation of the Council, on February 16, 1889, granted the Bishop of Bayonne permission, for a period of ten years, to admit to the diocesan synod procurators selected by the pastors of each deanery as their representatives, this was an exception made because of the large number of parishes in the dioçese and because of the great distance at which many of the pastors lived from the episcopal city.[13]

In that same year, basing their action on the decision of the Congregation in the above case, two other bishops applied for the same permission and both were refused, the Bishop of Brixen on July 6, 1889,[14] and the Bishop of Milwaukee on July 29, 1889.[15] The latter, asking that the rectors of missions from each deanery in his jurisdiction be permitted to choose two or three procurators as their representatives at the synod, gave as the reasons for not having all in attendance that some must be left in the churches to care for the needs of the faithful and, secondly, that

[11] Can. 21 — Mansi XXII, 1007-1010; c. 12, X, *de poenitentiis et remissionibus*, V, 38.

[12] Can. 362. Cf. Benedictus XIV, *De Synodo Dioecesana*, lib. III, c. 12, n. 4; lib. I, c. 2, n. 5; Wernz, *Ius Decretalium*, II, n. 860.

[13] *ASS*, XXI (1888), 726-729.

[14] *ASS*, XXII (1889-1890), 350-355.

[15] *Fontes*, n. 4922.

there were insufficient accommodations in the synodal city to care for all the rectors. The Congregation, in refusing the permission, suggested that the bishop summon to the synod all who in his judgment could be called without too great hardship.[16]

Article 2. Canonical Elections

Canon 163 rules that votes may not be cast by a proxy in canonical elections unless a particular law permits such a practice. Immediately prior to the Code the same prohibition applied to elections in religious institutes, but not to those in other collegiate bodies; in fact at one time the use of proxies was permitted generally.

The I Ecumenical Council (I Nicaea, 325) prescribed that all the bishops of a province were to elect a candidate to fill a vacant see in the same province. Any bishop prevented from attending was to send his consent by a procurator.[17]

In its chapter on canonical elections, later included in the Decretals of Gregory IX,[18] the XII Ecumenical Council (IV Lateran, 1215) legislated against the use of procurators in voting except under two conditions; namely, that the elector had to be in a place where he had a right to be informed of the forthcoming election, and that he was prevented by a serious reason from assisting at the election.[19]

---

[16] It is interesting to note that the privilege which these bishops requested and which only one received is now, in essence, part of the universal law, being contained in canon 358, § 1, 7°. But the pastor so chosen can hardly be called a procurator; for, by the fact of his election, he has the right to assist at the synod in his own name.

[17] Can. 4 — Mansi, II, 701. This canon is incorporated in the *Decretum Gratiani,* c. 1, D. LXIV. Cf. c. 3, D. LXV.

[18] C. 42, X, *de electione et potestate electi,* I, 6.

[19] Can. 24 — Mansi, XXII, 1011. As to how far from the place of the election an elector had to be before he lost the right to be notified and hence to name a procurator, the general norm seems to have been based on the ability of the absent elector to arrive at the time set for the election. Cf. Schmalzgrueber, lib. I, tit. VI, n. 27; Piat, *Praelectiones Iuris Regularis* (2. ed., 2 voll., Parisiis, 1888), I, 501. According to Reiffenstuel (lib. I, tit. VI, n. 182) custom helped to determine this.

A chapter in the *Liber Sextus*[20] made some further restrictions on the use of a procurator in elections; namely,

1) a non-member of the electoral body could be appointed as procurator only if the body consented;

2) several proxies could be appointed, but each was to be appointed *in solidum*; otherwise none was to be admitted;

3) if there were several, the one chosen by the majority of the electoral body was to be admitted; if none was agreed on, he who first presented his mandate was to be accepted;

4) if the proxy was already an elector he could cast one vote for each of two candidates only if the mandator had specifically designated his choice; if the proxy was left free in his choice and thereupon cast one vote for each of two candidates, neither vote counted.[21]

The Council of Trent forbade the use of proxies in elections held by religious institutes; a violation of this decree rendered the election null.[22] It will be noted that the Council in the matter of elections made an exception in regard to religious, but added to its decree no clause abrogating contrary privileges or constitutional provisions. Hence Castellini (†1631) argued that the Council did not absolutely forbid the use of proxies in the election of religious

---

[20] C. 46, *de electione et potestate electi*, I, 6, in VI°.

[21] The glossator of the same chapter (ad. v. "nihil agit") gives the reason for the last provision; "Ratio est quia qua conscientia tenetur meliorem eligere suo nomine; eadem ratione tenetur ad idem nomine domini sui." Hostiensis, although admitting the reasonableness of such a view, had held the contrary opinion: "Puto contrarium, dummodo neuter sit malus, sed tunc diminuitur numerus vocis suae. Honestius est etiam quod consentiat in eamdem personam." —*Commentaria*, lib. I, tit. VI, *de electione et potestate electi*, n. 63e.

Coronota maintains, and rightly so, that the same holds true today; that is, in elections in which by reason of a particular law proxies are permitted to be used, an elector who is casting a vote for another elector and is simultaneously authorized to exercise his own choice must cast both votes for the same candidate. —*Compendium Iuris Canonici* (2 voll., Taurini: Ex Officina Libraria Marietti, 1937), I, 289.

[22] Sess. XXV, *de regularibus*, c. 6.

superiors, but permitted the constitutions of the particular institutes to be followed.[23]

Indeed, the Constitution "Christifidelium," issued by Pope Innocent XII (1691-1700) on February 16, 1694, explicitly permitted religious to follow the provisions of their constitutions in this matter.[24] Innocent XIII (1721-1724) maintained the prohibition against proxy-voters in elections held in religious institutes when he refused the minister-general of an order permission to supply the votes of electors who were prevented by serious causes from assisting at an election.[25]

A decree of the Congregation of Bishops and Regulars, on March 11, 1836, to the Minister General of the whole Order of Franciscan Minors, provided that when the constitutions of the institute did not permit proxy-electors, then absent members of the general chapter could not appoint procurators even to assist at the chapter, although no attempt to claim a vote was made.[26]

That the right to appoint a proxy in elections of other collegiate bodies remained unaltered after the Council of Trent is clear from a decision of the Roman Rota which sustained an election wherein a procurator participated.[27] Galliher, writing shortly before the publication of the Code, stated the general principle: "All absent electors can elect a procurator unless prohibited by particular statute.[28] A prohibitory statute did exist, of

---

[23] *De Electione Canonica* (Romae, 1625), p. 163, n. 98. Cf. Parsons, *Canonical Elections,* The Catholic University of America Canon Law Studies, n. 118 (Washington, D. C.: The Catholic University of America Press, 1939), p. 74.

[24] § 12 — *Fontes,* n. 257.

[25] S. C. Ep. et Reg., *Ordinis Minorum Observantium,* 15 maii 1723 — *Fontes,* n. 1840.

[26] *Fontes,* n. 1909.

[27] *Leodien.* 10 dec. 1677 — *Sacrae Rotae Romanae Decisiones Recentiores,* Pars XIX, tom. I (ab Ioanne Baptista Compagno comp., Romae, 1682), p. 235, dec. CXLI.

"Absentes propter legitimum impedimentum ex iuris communis concessione per procuratorem quasi praesentes esse et eligere possunt." — Wernz, *Ius Decretalium,* II, n. 358.

[28] *Canonical Elections,* The Catholic University of America Canon Law Studies, n. 2 (Washington, D. C., 1917), p. 37.

course, in regard to elections held in religious institutes, so that a presumption was established against the use of procurators in such elections. But this was an exception to the general law. Now, by the law of the Code, the exception has become the rule: votes cast by proxies in any canonical election are null, unless a particular law rules otherwise.

An understanding of the meaning of the phrase, "a particular law," is important in the interpretation of canon 163. Is this to be restricted to laws promulgated by the Holy See for a particular electoral college? Is only written law to be included? Michiels very succinctly summarizes the interpretation to be placed on this and similar phrases contained in the canons dealing with elections:[29] "Ad naturam iuris particularis quod spectat, omnino retinendum videtur, propter generalia clausulae verba, approbari in hac materia quodlibet ius particulare, sive scriptum sive etiam consuetudinarium, sive ante Codicis promulgationem vigens sive postea legitime introductum."[30] Toso is equally broad in his interpretation.[31] In his dissertation on canonical elections, Parsons treats of this subject at great length and arrives at the same conclusion; that is, by the term "lex peculiaris" must be understood written or customary law, promulgated before or after the Code, by the Holy See or by an inferior legislator. He stresses the fact, however, that the provision must be a stable act of legislation, not merely a temporary arrangement in a particular instance. Only the Holy See could permit this.[32]

This interpretation is not accepted unanimously. Augustine (†1943) denies the validity of customary law in this respect, saying that the Code "speaks of laws enacted in a special man-

[29] E. g., "nisi aliter particularibus legibus vel legitimis consuetudinibus fuerit constitutum" — can. 168; "nisi aliud in iure caveatur" — cans. 172, § 1; 177, § 4.

[30] *Principia Generalia De Personis in Ecclesia* (Lublin: Universitas Catholica, 1932), pp. 392-393.

[31] "Lex particularis, quam Codex hic expresse reservat, esse potest lex fundationis, religionis statuta aut ius particulare quomodocumque legitime introductum." — *Ad Codicem Iuris Canonici Commentaria*, Lib. II, *De Personis*, tom. I (Romae, 1922), p. 133.

[32] *Canonical Elections*, pp. 89-90; 111-112.

ner."[33] DeMeester, in his commentary on canon 101, § 1, 1°, excludes customary law from the phrase "nisi aliud expresse iure communi aut particulari statutum fuerit."[34] Evidently he would apply the same interpretation to the exceptive clause of canon 163, since canon 101 deals with all acts of moral collegiate persons. Maroto (1875-1937) [35] and Ayrinhac (1867-1930) [36] while admitting the force of custom in permitting the use of procurators in elections, deny that any legislator less than the Holy See can promulgate a law permitting such a practice.[37]

Such restrictive interpretations lack any intrinsic authority, and hence it must be concluded with the canonists cited above that the use of procurators in canonical elections may be granted by written or customary law, issued by the Holy See or an inferior legislator, promulgated before or after the Code.

Parsons decides in the affirmative two questions on this subject as regards inferior legislators acting after the Code:

1) may an ordinary, in drawing up constitutions for a new diocesan institute, insert a clause permitting the use of proxies in elections?

---

[33] [Bachofen], Charles Augustine, *A Commentary on the New Code of Canon Law* (8 vols., St. Louis, 1918-1921), II, 128. The same author *(loc. cit.)* states: "The Decretals as well as the Tridentine Council and several decisions of the Roman Curia had forbidden voting by proxy." It has already been shown (*supra,* p. 67) that this applied only to religious institutes.

Coronata, in his discussion of the force of custom, refers to the clause in canon 163, "nisi lege peculiari aliud caveatur," as an example of a law *requiring,* not merely *permitting,* the use of a contrary custom.—*Compendium Iuris Canonici,* I, 128.

[34] *Iuris Canonici et Iuris Canonico-Civilis Compendium* (3 voll. in 4, nova editio, Brugis, 1921-1928), I, 222, *nota* 1.

[35] *Institutiones Iuris Canonici,* I, 746.

[36] *General Legislation in the New Code of Canon Law* (New York: Longmans, Green and Co., 1933), p. 332.

[37] Ayrinhac, commenting *(loc. cit.)* on canon 163, writes: "Contrary laws have been abrogated. (Can. 6, 1°)." But the exceptive clause in canon 6, 1°, "nisi de particularibus legibus aliud expresse caveatur," has application to canon 163, which contains the clause, "nisi lege peculiari aliud caveatur." Hence particular laws contrary to canon 163 are not abrogated.

2) may the general chapter of a religious institute, which has the power to change its constitutions without the intervention of the Holy See, adopt a law permitting their use? He warns, however, in the former case, that it would be unwise to take advantage of the exception in the law if papal approbation of the institute is hoped for eventually.[38]

If a particular law permits the employment of procurators at elections, the details as to who may choose one (any absent elector or only those prevented by sickness, etc.) and who may be chosen (members or non-members of the collegiate body, etc.) will be determined in the particular law. If one who is already an elector is named, he will have, of course, two votes. The restriction to one vote by an elector who has the right to vote on several titles applies only if the titles are to be exercised in his own name.[39]

If the electors of a collegiate body not governed by such a law deliberately admit the vote of a proxy, they are subject to the penalty to be imposed by the ordinary.[40] If the proxy were not a member of the body, the election would be null, whether or not the electors were aware of the illegality of their action.[41]

Article 3. The Profession of Faith

Those obliged to make a profession of faith[42] do not satisfy their obligation by the use of a procurator in making it.[43] In this the Code maintains the discipline which has been recognized since the Council of Trent prescribed the profession of faith,[44] as several responses of the Sacred Congregation of the Council show.[45] Moreover, any contrary custom is reprobated.[46]

---

38 *Canonical Elections,* p. 90.

39 Can. 164.

40 Can. 2391, § 2: "Singuli vero electores qui substantialem electionis formam scienter non servaverint, possunt pro gravitate culpae ab Ordinario puniri."

41 Can. 165; can. 16, § 1.

42 Can. 1406 lists those who are so obliged.

43 Can. 1407.

44 Sess. XXIV, *de ref.,* c. 12.

45 S. C. C., *Panormitana,* mense maio 1586—*Fontes,* n. 2157; *Valentina,* 5 febr. 1611—*Fontes,* n. 2387; *Calaguritana,* 22 sept. 1696—*Fontes,* n. 2954; *Cathacen.,* 26 ian., 9 febr. 1726—*Fontes,* n. 3310.

46 Can. 1408. Blat rightly asserts that the ordinary cannot dispense from this law.—*Commentarium Textus Codicis Iuris Canonici,* III, 327.

At one time, however, canonists of no mean repute argued in favor of such a practice.[47] Thus Barbosa (1589-1649) approved of the use of a proxy in making the profession of faith, although he cited a number of opponents of this opinion.[48] Relying on this author, and denying the issuance of any replies to the contrary by the Sacred Congregation of the Council, Reiffenstuel (1641-1703) maintained the same view.[49] But certainly there was no obscurity in the above-cited replies of the Sacred Congregation, and hence the acquiescence of all canonists eventually followed the promulgation of these responses.[50]

The use of a procurator for the profession of faith required in taking possession of a benefice, while not rendering possession invalid, since the profession is not necessary for valid possession, would deprive the beneficiary of the right to the fruits of the benefice and make him liable to the other penalties of canon 2403.[51]

Article 4. The Taking of an Oath

Another exception to the use of a procurator is made by canon 1316, § 2: "Iusiurandum quod canones exigunt vel admittunt, per procuratorem praestari valide nequit."

This exception rests solely on positive law, for there was a time when even the act of taking an oath could be accomplished through another. In a letter of Pope John VIII (872-882) to Willibert, Archbishop of Cologne, in the year 873, reference is made to an oath by proxy. In his letter the pope stated four

---

[47] Cf. Canavan, *Profession of Faith,* The Catholic University of America Canon Law Studies, n. 151 (Washington, D. C.: The Catholic University of America Press, 1942), p. 54.

[48] *Ius Ecclesiasticum Universum* (3 voll., Lugduni, 1650), lib. I, c. XXI, n. 56. Apparently the question became the object of heated controversy, for Barbosa complained of Sigismundus à Bononomia (1587-1632) as "parum modeste et religiose de me loquentem" in this dispute.

[49] Lib. I, tit. I, n. 181-187.

[50] Cf. Wernz, *Ius Decretalium,* III, n. 18.

[51] This was precisely the case presented to the Sacred Congregation of the Council by the Bishop of Palmero. The cathedral canons had made the profession of faith through proxies. The Congregation ruled that not only was this act of no account, and that the profession was to be made personally, but that the canons were not entitled to the fruits already received. — S. C. C., *Panormitana,* mense maio 1586 — *Fontes,* n. 2157.

reasons for refusing the pallium to Willibert, one of which was that the latter had sent no one to the Holy See to take the oath for him.[52]

The oath of Otto I (936-973) to Pope John XII (955-964), in the year 962, whereby he swore to protect the pontiff and the possessions of the Church in Rome, furnishes a famous example of an oath by proxy, for Otto did not appear in person at the Holy See, but sent a procurator to swear in his name.[53]

But now the law of the Code is to the contrary, so that any oath required or admitted by the Code must be taken personally.

The exception contained in canon 1746 is to be applied to the obligation of appearing before the judge, not to the obligation of personally taking an oath and testifying.[54] The oath that a procurator takes when he receives the pallium for a metropolitan, as is permitted by canon 275, is not in the name of his principal but in his own name, to the effect that he will be faithful to his duty of delivering the pallium to the archbishop.[55]

---

[52] C. 4, D. C; Jaffé, n. 2986; Mansi, XVII, 242; *MPL*, CXXVI, 652. The Friedberg edition of the *Corpus Iuris Canonici* refers to n. 2245 in the first edition of Jaffé. It should read, n. 2244.

[53] C. 33, D. LXIII. The glossator mentioned that even if the principal recalled his mandate to take an oath, he was nevertheless bound by it if notice of the revocation failed to reach the procurator before the oath had been taken.—*Glossa* ad v. "et iurare." Cf. c. 32, C. XVII, q. 4; *glossa* of Reg. 68, R. J., in VI°. Schmalzgrueber (lib. II, tit. XXIV, n. 81) attested to the continued validity of the practice.

[54] "Ad iusiurandum praestandum vel interrogationibus respondendum partes personaliter coram iudice se sistere debent, exceptis iis de quibus in can. 1770, § 2, nn. 1, 2."

[55] The formula for this oath is contained in the Constitution *"Rerum ecclesiasticarum"* of Pope Benedict XIV, issued on August 12, 1748—*Fontes*, n. 390. The ceremony when a procurator is used is described in the Constitution *"Inter conspicuas,"* issued by the same pontiff on August 29, 1744—*Fontes*, n. 347.

Catalani (†after 1757) is authority for the statement that the practice of using a procurator for the reception of the pallium was admitted by the Holy See as early as the twelfth century.—*Pontificale Romanum Clementis VIII ac Urbani VIII*, Vol. I (nova ed., auctore Iosepho Catalano, Parisiis, 1850), p. 386; tit., *De Pallio*, § I, n. 2.

SCHOLION

PRECEDENCE

Canon 106, § 1, lays down the principle that one acting for another occupies the latter's position in the matter of precedence. An exception is made, however, in regard to councils and other similar gatherings, whereby a procurator follows all those who are of the same rank as the principal whom he represents.[1]

[1] "Sacerdos qui in Concilio Plenario interest ut Archiepiscopi procurator, sedet post Archiepiscopos, sed ante Episcopos." — Moretti, *Ceremoniale Iuxta Ritum Romanum, seu de Sacris Functionibus,* Vol. I, *De Quibusdam Notionibus Sacram Liturgiam Respicientibus* (Taurini: Officina Libraria Marietti, 1936), p. 71.

CONCLUSIONS

1. The ecclesiastical office of procurator was adopted by the Church from Roman law.

2. The general principles governing the use of procurators are found in the *Regulae Juris*.

3. The institution of agency in American and English law is attributed to that of procuratorship in canon law.

4. The institution of procuratorship, though it gave rise to many ecclesiastical offices, is of much less importance today in canon law than formerly. It is to be included in the term "ecclesiastical office" in a broad sense, not having to do with the exercise of jurisdiction.

5. Procurators can be used in all matters unless their use is prohibited by positive law or by the nature of the case.

6. The use of extra-judicial procurators is found most frequently in the administration of the sacraments of baptism, confirmation and matrimony, and in the celebration of councils.

BIBLIOGRAPHY

Sources

Acta Apostolicae Sedis, Commentarium Officiale, Romae, 1909—

Acta et Decreta Concilii Plenarii I Australasiae, Sydney, 1887.

Acta et Decreta Concilii Plenarii Baltimorensis Tertii, Baltimorae, 1886.

Acta et Decreta Concilii Provincialis Portlandensis in Oregon Quarti, Portlandiae, 1934.

Acta Sanctae Sedis, 41 voll., Romae, 1865-1908.

Canones et Decreta Concilii Tridentini, Taurini, 1913.

Codex Iuris Canonici Pii X Pontificis Maximi iussu digestus Benedicti Papae XV auctoritate promulgatus, Romae: Typis Polyglottis Vaticanis, 1917.

Codicis Iuris Canonici Fontes, cura Emi. Petri Card. Gasparri editi, 9 voll., Romae (postea Civitate Vaticana): Typis Polyglottis Vaticanis, 1923-1939. (Voll. VII-IX, ed. cura et studio Emi. Iustiniani Card. Serédi).

Collectanea S. Congregationis De Propaganda Fide, 2 voll., Romae, 1907.

Collectio Lacensis, 7 voll., Friburgi Brisgoviae, 1870-1890.

Collectio Librorum Iuris Ante-Iustiniani, 3 voll. in 2, ed. Krueger, Mommsen, Studemund, Berolini, 1878.

Collectio Omnium Conclusionum et Resolutionum quae in causis propositis apud Sacram Congregationem Cardinalium S. Concilii Tridentini Interpretum prodierunt ab anno 1564 ad annum 1860, cura et studio Salvatoris Pallottini, 18 voll., Romae, 1868-1895.

Concilia Provincialia Baltimori habita ab anno 1829 usque ad annum 1849, edito altera, Baltimori, 1851.

Concilii Plenarii Baltimorensis II Acta et Decreta, editio altera mendis expurgata, Baltimorae, 1894.

Concilii Tridentini Diariorum, Actorum, Epistularum, Tractatuum Nova Collectio, 13 voll., ed. Societas Goerresiana, Friburgi Brisgoviae: B. Herder, 1901-1938.

Concilium Baltimorense Provinciale IX, Baltimori, 1858.

Corpus Iuris Canonici, editio Lipsiensis II post Aemilii Ludovici Richteri curas instruxit Aemilius Friedberg, 1879-1881. Editio anastatice repetita, Lipsiae: Tauchnitz, 1922.

Corpus Iuris Civilis, 3 voll., Berolini: Apud Weidmannos, 1928-1929.

Decreta Authentica Congregationis Sacrorum Rituum ex actis eiusdem collecta eiusque auctoritate promulgata sub auspiciis SS. D. N. Leonis Papae XIII, 5 voll. et appendix, Romae, 1898-1912.

Denziger, H.-Bannwart, C.-Umberg, I. B., *Enchiridion Symbolorum Definitionum et Declarationum de Rebus Fidei et Morum*, 6. et 7. ed., Friburgi Brisgoviae: Herder et Co., 1928.

Jaffé, Ph., *Regesta Pontificum Romanorum ab condita Ecclesia ad annum post Christum natum MCXCVIII*, 2. ed., 2 voll., Lipsiae, 1885-1888.

Louisiana Civil Code, 1932.

Mansi, Ioannes, *Sacrorum Conciliorum Nova et Amplissima Collectio,* 53 voll. in 59, Parisiis, 1901-1927.

Potthast, Augustus, *Regesta Pontificum Romanorum inde ab anno post Christum natum MCXCVIII ad MCCCIV,* 2 voll., Berolini, 1874-1875.

Sacrae Romanae Rotae Decisiones seu Sententiae, Romae, 1909—

Sacrae Rotae Romanae Decisiones Recentiores, Pars XIX, tom. I, ab Ioanne Baptista Compagno compilatae, Romae, 1682.

Sanctae Rotae Romanae Decisiones coram Molines, 5 voll., Romae, 1728.

Thesaurus Resolutionum Sacrae Congregationis Concilii, 167 voll., Romae, 1718-1908.

Reference Works

Albertario, Emilio, *Procurator Unius Rei,* Pavia, 1921.

Alford, Culver B., *Jus Civile Matrimoniale in Statibus Foederatis Americae Septentrionalis Cum Jure Canonico Comparatum,* Roma: Anonima Libraria Cattolica Italiana, 1938.

Allshorn, Lionel, *Stupor Mundi*: *Life and Times of Frederick II,* London, 1912.

Ayrinhac, H. A., *General Legislation in the New Code of Canon Law,* New York: Longmans, Green and Co., 1933.

————, *Marriage Legislation in the New Code of Canon Law,* revised and enlarged by P. J. Lydon, revised edition, New York: Benziger Bros., 1935.

[Bachofen], Charles Augustine, *A Commentary on the New Code of Canon Law,* 8 vols., St. Louis, 1918-1921.

Barbosa, Augustinus, *De Officio et Potestate Episcopi,* Lugduni, 1666.

————, *Ius Ecclesiasticum Universum,* 3 voll., Lugduni, 1650.

————, *Summa Apostolicarum Decisionum,* Lugduni, 1685.

Benedictus XIV, *De Synodo Dioecesana,* 2 voll., Parmae, 1764.

Berardi, Aemilius, *Theologia Moralis,* 5 voll., Faventiae, 1905.

Bernardus Papiensis, *Summa Decretalium,* ed. E. A. Th. Layspeyres, Ratisbonae, 1860.

Billot, Ludovicus, *De Ecclesiae Sacramentis,* 7. ed., 2 voll., Romae: Aedes Universitatis Gregorianae, 1929-1931.

Blackstone, Sir William, *Commentaries on the Laws of England,* edited with notes by William G. Hammond, 4 vols., San Francisco, 1890.

Blat, Albertus, *Commentarium Textus Codicis Iuris Canonici,* 5 voll. in 6, Romae, 1920-1927.

Bouix, Dominique, *De Concilio Provinciali,* 2. ed., Parisiis, 1862.

————, *De Papa et de Concilio Oecumenico,* 3 voll., Parisiis, 1870.

Buckland, W. W., *A Text-Book of Roman Law,* 2. ed., Cambridge: The University Press, 1932.

Burdick, William L., *The Principles of Roman Law and Their Relation to Modern Law,* Rochester, N. Y.: The Lawyers' Co-operative Publishing Co., 1938.

Caietanus, Thomas, *Opuscula Omnia,* Venetiis, 1588.

Cambridge Medieval History, The, 8 vols., edited by J. R. Tanner, C. W. Previté-Orton and Z. N. Brooke, New York: Macmillan Co., 1911-1936.

Canavan, Walter J., *The Profession of Faith,* The Catholic University of America Canon Law Studies, n. 151, Washington, D. C.: The Catholic University of America Press, 1942.

Cano, Melchior, *Opera,* Bassani, 1746.

Capitula Angilramni, apud Decretales Pseudo-Isidorianae et Capitula Angilramni, ed. Paulus Hinschius, Lipsiae, 1863.

Cappello, Felix M., *Tractatus Canonico-Moralis de Sacramentis,* Vol. I, 2. ed. emendata et aucta, Taurinorum Augustae: Officina Libraria Marietti, 1928; Vol. III, 4. ed. emendata et aucta, Taurinorum Augustae: Officina Libraria Marietti, 1939.

Castellini, Luca, *De Electione Canonica,* Romae, 1625.

Catalani, Iosephus, *Pontificale Romanum Clementis VIII ac Urbani VIII,* Vol. I, nova editio, Parisiis, 1850.

Cencius, Ludovicus, *Tractatus De Procuratoribus,* opus posthumum a Petro Hyeronimo Cencio adauctum et illustratum, Florentiae, 1857.

Collegii Salmanticensis Theologia Moralis, 4 voll., Venetiis, 1714.

Concina, Danielis, *Theologia Christiana Dogmatico-Moralis,* 10 voll., Romae, 1749-1751.

Coninck, Aegidius, *Commentarium in Universam Doctrinam D. Thomae de Sacramentis et Censuris,* 2 voll. in 1, Antverpiae, 1619.

Coronata, Matthaeus, Conte A, *Compendium Iuris Canonici,* 2 voll., Taurini: Ex Officina Libraria Marietti, 1937.

———, *Institutiones Iuris Canonici,* 5 voll., Taurini: Ex Officina Libraria Marietti, 1928-1936.

De Luca, Ioannes Baptista, *Theatrum Veritatis et Iustitiae,* 16 voll., Coloniae Agrippinae, 1706.

De Lugo, Ioannes, *Disputationes Scholasticae et Morales,* 8 voll., Parisiis, 1869.

De Meester, A., *Iuris Canonici et Iuris Canonico-Civilis Compendium,* 3 voll. in 4, nova editio, Brugis, 1921-1928.

Dictionary of National Biography, 63 vols., New York, 1885-1900.

DuCange, *Glossarium Mediae et Infimae Latinitatis,* conditum a Carolo du Fresne Domino du Cange, auctum a monachis Ordinis S. Benedicti cum supplementis integris D. P. Carpenterii, digessit G. A. L. Henschel, Vol. VI, Paris: Libraire des Sciences et des Arts, 1938.

Durandus [Duranti], Gulielmus, *Speculum Iuris,* Venetiis, 1577.

Engel, Ludovicus, *Collegium Iuris Canonici,* Beneventi, 1760.

Esmein, Adhemar, *Le Mariage en Droit Canonique,* 2. ed., par R. Génestal et Jean Dauvillier, 2 vols., Paris: Libraire du Recueil Sirey, 1929-1935.

Eubel, C., *Hierarchia Catholica Medii Aevi,* 2. ed., 4 voll., Monasterii, 1913-1935.

Fagnanus, Prosper, *Commentaria in Quinque Libros Decretalium,* 5 voll., Venetiis, 1709.

Ferraris, F. Lucius, *Prompta Bibliotheca, Canonica, Iuridica, Moralis, Theologica, necnon Ascetica, Polemica, Rubricistica, Historica*, 9 voll., Romae, 1885-1899.

Fournier, Edouard, *Les Origines du Vicaire-Général*, Paris, 1922.

———, *Le Vicaire-Général au Moyen-Age*, Paris, 1923.

Froude, James Anthony, *History of England from the Fall of Wolsey to the Death of Elizabeth*, 6 vols., London, 1860.

Galliher, Daniel M., *Canonical Elections*, The Catholic University of America Canon Law Studies, n. 2, Washington, D. C., 1917.

Gasparri, Petrus, *De Matrimonio*, 2. ed., 2 voll., Parisiis, 1892.

———, *Tractatus Canonicus de Matrimonio*, editio nova ad mentem Codicis I. C., 2 voll., Romae: Typis Polyglottis Vaticanis, 1932.

Graesse, G. Th., *Orbis Latinus*, 2. ed., Berolini, 1909.

Gutierrez, Ioannes, *Quaestiones Canonicae*, 3 voll., Noribergae, 1647.

Hefele, Charles Joseph et LeClercq, Henri, *Histoire des Conciles*, 10 vols. in 19, Paris: Libraire Letouzey et Ané, 1907-1938.

Hogan, James J., *Judicial Advocates and Procurators*, The Catholic University of America Canon Law Studies, n. 133, Washington, D. C.: The Catholic University of America Press, 1941.

Hostiensis, Henricus, *In Libros Decretalium Commentaria*, 5 voll. in 3, Venetiis, 1581.

———, *Summa Aurea*, Venetiis, 1570.

Kieda, Franciscus, *De Matrimonii Celebratione Per Procuratorem*, Romae: Typis Pontificiae Universitatis Gregorianae, 1939.

Ledesma, Petrus de, *De Magno Matrimonii Sacramento*, Venetiis, 1595.

Lucidi, Angelus, *De Visitatione Sanctorum Liminum Instructio S. C. Concilii*, edita iussu S. M. Benedicti XIII, 3. ed. per Iosephum Schneider, 3 voll., Romae, 1883.

Marcus, Georgius, *Per Procuratorem Quomodo Iure Romano et Hodierno Obligationes Contrahuntur*, Berolini, 1872.

Maroto, Philippus, *Institutiones Iuris Canonici ad Normam Novi Codicis*, 2 voll., Matriti, 1919.

Matthaei Parisiensis Chronica Majora, 7 voll., ed. by Henry Richards Luard, London, 1876-1883.

Maynz, Charles, *Cours de Droit Romain*, 3. ed., 3 vols., Paris, 1870-1874.

Mechem, Floyd R., *Outlines of the Law of Agency*, 3. ed., Chicago, 1923.

Michiels, Gommarus, *Principia Generalia De Personis in Ecclesia*, Lublin: Universitas Catholica, 1932.

Migne, Jacques-Paul, *Patrologiae Cursus Completus, Series Latina*, 221 voll., Parisiis, 1844-1864.

Moretti, Aloisius, *Ceremoniale iuxta Ritum Romanum seu de Sacris Functionibus*, Vol. I, *De Quibusdam Notionibus Sacram Liturgiam Respicientibus*, Taurini: Officina Libraria Marietti, 1936.

Noldin, H., *Summa Theologiae Moralis*, Vol. III, *De Sacramentis*, 25. ed., recognovit et emendavit A. Schmitt, Oeniponte/Lipsiae: Felicianus Rauch, 1938.

Pallavicini, Sfortia, *Vera Concilii Tridentini Historia*, 3 voll., Antverpiae, 1670.

Panormitanus, Abbas [Nicholas de Tudeschis], *Commentaria in Quinque Decretalium Libros*, 8 voll., Venetiis, 1588.

Parsons, Anscar, *Canonical Elections*, The Catholic University of America Canon Law Studies, n. 118, Washington, D. C.: The Catholic University of America Press, 1939.

Payen, G., *De Matrimonio in Missionibus*, Vol. II, Zi-Ka-Wei: Typographia T'oo-Sè-Wè, 1929.

Petrovits, Joseph J. C., *The New Church Law of Matrimony*, 2. revised ed., Philadelphia: John Joseph McVey, 1926.

Piat, F., *Praelectiones Iuris Regularis*, 2. ed., 2 voll., Parisiis, 1888.

Pirhing, Ernricus, *Ius Canonicum in Quinque Libris Decretalium*, 5 voll. in 4, Dilingae, 1677.

Pistocchi, Marius, *De Re Beneficiali iuxta Canones*, Taurini: Officina Libraria Marietti, 1928.

Quintana, Manuel Jose, *La Vida de Vasco Nuñez de Balboa*, edited by George Griffin Brownell, Boston, 1914.

S. Raymundus Peñafort, *Summa*, Veronae, 1744.

Reiffenstuel, Anacletus, *Ius Canonicum Universum*, 5 voll. in 4, Venetiis, 1735.

Riganti, Ioannes Baptista, *Commentaria in Regulas, Constitutiones et Ordinationes Cancellariae Apostolicae*, 2 voll., Coloniae Allobrogum, 1751.

Rufinus, *Die Summa Decretorum des Magister Rufinus*, ed. Heinrich Singer, Paderborn, 1902.

Sanchez, Thomas, *De Sancto Matrimonii Sacramento*, Antverpiae, 1626.

Scavini, Petrus, *Theologia Moralis Universa*, 3 voll., Mediolani, 1860.

Schiappoli, Domenico, *Il Matrimonio Secondo Il Diritto Canonico e La Legislazione Concordataria Italiana*, Napoli: L. Alvano, 1932.

Schmalzgrueber, Franciscus, *Ius Ecclesiasticum Universum*, 5 voll. in 12, Romae, 1843-1845.

Schouler, James, *A Treatise on the Law of Marriage, Divorce, Separation and Domestic Relations*, 6. ed., by Arthur W. Blakemore, 3 vols., Albany, N. Y., 1921, vol. I, *The Law of Marriage and Divorce*.

Slaughter, Gertrude, *The Amazing Frederick*, New York: Macmillan Co., 1937.

Smith, S. B., *Elements of Ecclesiastical Law*, Vol. I, *Ecclesiastical Persons*, 5. ed., New York, 1883.

———————— 9. ed., New York, 1887.

Suarez, Franciscus, *Opera Omnia*, 26 voll., editio nova a Carlo Berton, Parisiis, 1856-1866.

Thomassinus, Ludovicus, *Vetus et Nova Ecclesiae Disciplina*, 10 voll., Magontiaci, 1787.

Toso, Albertus, *Ad Codicem Iuris Canonici Commentaria Minora*, lib. II, *De Personis*, tom. I, Romae, 1922.

Wernz, F. X., *Ius Decretalium*, 6 voll., Romae, 1898-1905.

Wernz, F. X., et Vidal, Petrus, *Ius Canonicum ad Codicis Normam Exactum*, vol. V, *Ius Matrimoniale*, Romae: apud Aedes Universitatis Gregorianae, 1925.

Woywod, Stanislaus, *A Practical Commentary on the Code of Canon Law*, 5. ed., revised, 2 vols., New York: Joseph F. Wagner, 1939.

PERIODICALS

Analecta Iuris Pontificii, Romae, 1855-1868; Parisiis, 1869-1891.

Apollinaris, Romae, 1928—

Conference Bulletin of the Archdiocese of New York, vol. XX, n. 1, (March, 1943).

Federal Reporter, St. Paul, Minn.

Harvard Law Review, Cambridge, Mass., 1887—

Jurist, The, Washington, D. C., 1941—

Southwest Reporter, St. Paul, Minn.

ABBREVIATIONS

AAS—Acta Apostolicae Sedis

ASS—Acta Sanctae Sedis

C—Codex Iustinianus

CBNY—Conference Bulletin of the Archdiocese of New York

D—Digesta Iustiniani

MPL—Migne, *Patrologiae Cursus Completus, Series Latina*

SRR Dec.—Sacrae Romanae Rotae Decisiones seu Sententiae.

ANALYTICAL INDEX

BIOGRAPHICAL NOTE

CHARLES PAUL CONNORS was born on October 30, 1912, in Pittsburgh, Pennsylvania. After completing the primary grades in St. Paul's Cathedral school and his high school studies in Duquesne University Preparatory School, he entered Duquesne University. Graduated with the degree of Bachelor of Arts in 1933, he entered the novitiate of the Holy Ghost Fathers at Ridgefield, Connecticut, where he made his religious profession on July 31, 1934. He began his theological studies at Ferndale, the Holy Ghost Fathers' Missionary Seminary at Norwalk, Connecticut, in the same year. On September 8, 1937, he was ordained to the priesthood, after which he continued his course in theology. In the fall of 1938 he entered the School of Canon Law of the Gregorian University, Rome, receiving the degree of Bachelor of Canon Law at the completion of the school term. After engaging in parish work in England during the summer of 1939, he was forced by the outbreak of the war to return to the United States, where he was appointed assistant at the parish of St. Mark the Evangelist, New York, and provincial secretary of the United States Province of the Holy Ghost Fathers. In October, 1942, he entered the Catholic University of America to continue his canon law studies and there received the degree of Licentiate in Canon Law in May, 1943.

CANON LAW STUDIES*

1. Freriks, Rev. Celestine A., C.PP.S., J.C.D., Religious Congregations in Their External Relations, 121 pp., 1916.
2. Galliher, Rev. Daniel M., O.P., J.C.D., Canonical Elections, 117 pp., 1917.
3. Borkowski, Rev. Aurelius L., O.F.M., J.C.D., De Confraternitatibus Ecclesiasticis, 136 pp., 1918.
4. Castillo, Rev. Cayo, J.C.D., Disertacion Historico-Canonica sobre la Potestad del Cabildo en Sede Vacante o Impedida del Vicario Capitular, 99 pp., 1919 (1918).
5. Kubelbeck, Rev. William J., S.T.B., J.C.D., The Sacred Penitentiaria and Its Relation to Faculties of Ordinaries and Priests, 129 pp., 1918.
6. Petrovits, Rev. Joseph, J.C., S.T.D., J.C.D., The New Church Law on Matrimony, X-461 pp., 1919.
7. Hickey, Rev. John J., S.T.B., J.C.D., Irregularities and Simple Impediments in the New Code of Canon Law, 100 pp., 1920.
8. Klekotka, Rev. Peter J., S.T.B., J.C.D., Diocesan Consultors, 179 pp., 1920.
9. Wanenmacher, Rev. Francis, J.C.D., The Evidence in Ecclesiastical Procedure Affecting the Marriage Bond, 1920 (Printed 1935).
10. Golden, Rev. Henry Francis, J.C.D., Parochial Benefices in the New Code, IV-119 pp., 1921 (Printed 1925).
11. Koudelka, Rev. Charles J., J.C.D., Pastors, Their Rights and Duties According to the New Code of Canon Law, 211 pp., 1921.
12. Melo, Rev. Antonius, O.F.M., J.C.D., De Exemptione Regularium, X-188 pp., 1921.
13. Schaaf, Rev. Valentine Theodore, O.F.M., S.T.B., J.C.D., The Cloister, X-180 pp., 1921.
14. Burke, Rev. Thomas Joseph, S.T.D., J.C.D., Competence in Ecclesiastical Tribunals, IV-117 pp., 1922.
15. Leech, Rev. George Leo, J.C.D., A Comparative Study of the Constitution "Apostolicae Sedis" and the "Codex Juris Canonici," 179 pp., 1922.
16. Motry, Rev. Hubert Louis, S.T.D., J.C.D., Diocesan Faculties According to the Code of Canon Law, II-167 pp., 1922.
17. Murphy, Rev. George Lawrence, J.C.D., Delinquencies and Penalties in the Administration and the Reception of the Sacraments, IV-121 pp., 1923.
18. O'Reilly, Rev. John Anthony, S.T.B., J.C.D., Ecclesiastical Sepulture in the New Code of Canon Law, II-129 pp., 1923.
19. Michalicka, Rev. Wenceslas Cyrill, O.S.B., J.C.D., Judicial Procedure in Dismissal of Clerical Exempt Religious, 107 pp., 1923.

* Below n. 100 only the following numbers are still available: Nn. 3, 4, 9, 25, 34, 57 and 75. Beginning with n. 100 only the following are unavailable: Nn. 100-111, inclusive, and n. 113.

20. Dargin, Rev. Edward Vincent, S.T.B., J.C.D., Reserved Cases According to the Code of Canon Law, IV-103 pp., 1924.
21. Godfrey, Rev. John A., S.T.B., J.C.D., The Right of Patronage According to the Code of Canon Law, 153 pp., 1924.
22. Hagedorn, Rev. Francis Edward, J.C.D., General Legislation on Indulgences, II-154 pp., 1924.
23. King, Rev. James Ignatius, J.C.D., The Administration of the Sacraments to Dying Non-Catholics, V-141 pp., 1924.
24. Winslow, Rev. Francis Joseph, O.F.M., J.C.D., Vicars and Prefects Apostolic, IV-149 pp., 1924.
25. Correa, Rev. Jose Servelion, S.T.L., J.C.D., La Potestad Legislativa de la Iglesia Catolica, IV-127 pp., 1925.
26. Dugan, Rev. Henry Francis, A.M., J.C.D., The Judiciary Department of the Diocesan Curia, 87 pp., 1925.
27. Keller, Rev. Charles Frederick, S.T.B., J.C.D., Mass Stipends, 167 pp., 1925.
28. Paschang, Rev. John Linus, J.C.D., The Sacramentals According to the Code of Canon Law, 129 pp., 1925.
29. Piontek, Rev. Cyrillus, O.F.M., S.T.B., J.C.D., De Indulto Exclaustrationis necnon Saecularizationis, XIII-289 pp., 1925.
30. Kearney, Rev. Richard Joseph, S.T.B., J.C.D., Sponsors at Baptism According to the Code of Canon Law, IV-127 pp., 1925.
31. Bartlett, Rev. Chester Joseph, A.M., LL.B., J.C.D., The Tenure of Parochial Property in the United States of America, V-108 pp., 1926.
32. Kilker, Rev. Adrian Jerome, J.C.D., Extreme Unction, V-425 pp., 1926.
33. McCormick, Rev. Robert Emmett, J.C.D., Confessors of Religious, VIII-266 pp., 1926.
34. Miller, Rev. Newton Thomas, J.C.D., Founded Masses According to the Code of Canon Law, VII-93 pp., 1926.
35. Roelker, Rev. Edward G., S.T.D., J.C.D., Principles of Privilege According to the Code of Canon Law, XI-166 pp., 1926.
36. Bakalarczyk, Rev. Richardus, M.I.C., J.U.D., De Novitiatu, VIII-208 pp., 1927.
37. Pizzuti, Rev. Lawrence, O.F.M., J.U.L., De Parochis Religiosis, 1927. (Not Printed).
38. Bliley, Rev. Nicholas Martin, O.S.B., J.C.D., Altars According to the Code of Canon Law, XIX-132 pp., 1927.
39. Brown, Mr. Brendan Francis, A.B., LL.M., J.U.D., The Canonical Juristic Personality with Special Reference to its Status in the United States of America, V-212 pp., 1927.
40. Cavanaugh, Rev. William Thomas, C.P., J.U.D., The Reservation of the Blessed Sacrament, VIII-101 pp., 1927.
41. Doheny, Rev. William J., C.S.C., A.B., J.U.D., Church Property: Modes of Acquisition, X-118 pp., 1927.

42. FELDHAUS, REV. ALOYSIUS H., C.PP.S., J.C.D., Oratories, IX-141 pp., 1927.
43. KELLY, REV. JAMES PATRICK, A.B., J.C.D., The Jurisdiction of the Simple Confessor, X-208 pp., 1927.
44. NEUBERGER, REV. NICHOLAS J., J.C.D., Canon 6 or the Relation of the Codex Juris Canonici to the Preceding Legislation, V-95 pp., 1927.
45. O'KEEFE, REV. GERALD MICHAEL, J.C.D., Matrimonial Dispensations, Powers of Bishops, Priests, and Confessors, VIII-232 pp., 1927.
46. QUIGLEY, REV. JOSEPH A. M., A.B., J.C.D., Condemned Societies, 139 pp., 1927.
47. ZAPLOTNIK, REV. JOHANNES LEO, J.C.D., De Vicariis Foraneis, X-142 pp., 1927.
48. DUSKIE, REV. JOHN ALOYSIUS, A.B., J.C.D., The Canonical Status of the Orientals in the United States, VIII-196 pp., 1928.
49. HYLAND, REV. FRANCIS EDWARD, J.C.D., Excommunication, Its Nature, Historical Development and Effects, VIII-181 pp., 1928.
50. REINMANN, REV. GERALD JOSEPH, O.M.C., J.C.D., The Third Order Secular of Saint Francis, 201 pp., 1928.
51. SCHENK, REV. FRANCIS J., J.C.D., The Matrimonial Impediments of Mixed Religion and Disparity of Cult, XVI-318 pp., 1929.
52. COADY, REV. JOHN JOSEPH, S.T.D., J.U.D., A.M., The Appointment of Pastors, VIII-150 pp., 1929.
53. KAY, REV. THOMAS HENRY, J.C.D., Competence in Matrimonial Procedure, VIII-164 pp., 1929.
54. TURNER, REV. SIDNEY JOSEPH, C.P., J.U.D., The Vow of Poverty, XLIX-217 pp., 1929.
55. KEARNEY, REV. RAYMOND A., A.B., S.T.D., J.C.D., The Principles of Delegation, VII-149 pp., 1929.
56. CONRAN, REV. EDWARD JAMES, A.B., J.C.D., The Interdict, V-163 pp., 1930.
57. O'NEILL, REV. WILLIAM H., J.C.D., Papal Rescripts of Favor, VII-218 pp., 1930.
58. BASTNAGEL, REV. CLEMENT VINCENT, J.U.D., The Appointment of Parochial Adjutants and Assistants, XV-257 pp., 1930.
59. FERRY, REV. WILLIAM A., A.B., J.C.D., Stole Fees, V-136 pp., 1930.
60. COSTELLO, REV. JOHN MICHAEL, A.B., J.C.D., Domicile and Quasi-Domicile, VII-201 pp., 1930.
61. KREMER, REV. MICHAEL NICHOLAS, A.B., S.T.B., J.C.D., Church Support in the United States, VI-136 pp., 1930.
62. ANGULA, REV. LUIS, C.M., J.C.D., Legislation de la Iglesia sobre la intencion en la application de la Santa Misa, VII-104 pp., 1931.
63. FREY, REV. WOLFGANG NORBERT, O.S.B., A.B., J.C.D., The Act of Religious Profession, VIII-174 pp., 1931.
64. ROBERTS, REV. JAMES BRENDAN, A.B., J.C.D., The Banns of Marriage, XIV-140 pp., 1931.

65. RYDER, REV. RAYMOND ALOYSIUS, A.B., J.C.D., Simony, IX-151 pp., 1931.
66. CAMPAGNA, REV. ANGELO, PH.D., J.U.D., Il Vicario Generale del Vescovo, VII-205 pp., 1931.
67. COX, REV. JOSEPH GODFREY, A.B., J.C.D., The Administration of Seminaries, VI-124 pp., 1931.
68. GREGORY, REV. DONALD J., J.U.D., The Pauline Privilege, XV-165 pp., 1931.
69. DONOHUE, REV. JOHN F., J.C.D., The Impediment of Crime, VII-110 pp., 1931.
70. DOOLEY, REV. EUGENE A., O.M.I., J.C.D., Church Law on Sacred Relics, IX-143 pp., 1931.
71. ORTH, REV. CLEMENT RAYMOND, O.M.C., J.C.D., The Approbation of Religious Institutes, 171 pp., 1931.
72. PERNICONE, REV. JOSEPH M., A.B., J.C.D., The Ecclesiastical Prohibition of Books, XII-267 pp., 1932.
73. CLINTON, REV. CONNELL, A.B., J.C.D., The Paschal Precept, IX-108 pp., 1932.
74. DONNELLY, REV. FRANCIS B., A.M., S.T.L., J.C.D., The Diocesan Synod, VIII-125 pp., 1932.
75. TORRENTE, REV. CAMILO, C.M.F., J.C.D., Las Processiones Sagradas, V-145 pp., 1932.
76. MURPHY, REV. EDWIN J., C.PP.S., J.C.D., Suspension Ex Informata Conscientia, XI-122 pp., 1932.
77. MACKENZIE, REV. ERIC F., A.M., S.T.L., J.C.D., The Delict of Heresy in its Commission, Penalization, Absolution, VII-124 pp., 1932.
78. LYONS, REV. AVITUS E., S.T.B., J.C.D., The Collegiate Tribunal of First Instance, XI-147 pp., 1932.
79. CONNOLLY, REV. THOMAS A., J.C.D., Appeals, XI-195 pp., 1932.
80. SANGMEISTER, REV. JOSEPH V., A.B., J.C.D., Force and Fear as Precluding Matrimonial Consent, V-211 pp., 1932.
81. JAEGER, REV. LEO A., A.B., J.C.D., The Administration of Vacant and Quasi-Vacant Episcopal Sees in the United States, IX-229 pp., 1932.
82. RIMLINGER, REV. HERBERT T., J.C.D., Error Invalidating Matrimonial Consent, VII-79 pp., 1932.
83. BARRETT, REV. JOHN D. M., S.S., J.C.D., A Comparative Study of the Third Plenary Council of Baltimore and the Code, IX-221 pp., 1932.
84. CARBERRY, REV. JOHN J., PH.D., S.T.D., J.C.D., The Juridical Form of Marriage, X-177 pp., 1934.
85. DOLAN, REV. JOHN L., A.B., J.C.D., The Defensor Vinculi, XII-157 pp., 1934.
86. HANNAN, REV. JEROME D., A.M., S.T.D., LL.B., J.C.D., The Canon Law of Wills, IX-517 pp., 1934.
87. LEMIEUX, REV. DELISE A., A.M., J.C.D., The Sentence in Ecclesiastical Procedure, IX-131 pp., 1934.

88. O'Rourke, Rev. James J., A.B., J.C.D., Parish Registers, VII-109 pp., 1934.
89. Timlin, Rev. Bartholomew, O.F.M., A.M., J.C.D., Conditional Matrimonial Consent, X-381 pp., 1934.
90. Wahl, Rev. Francis X., A.B., J.C.D., The Matrimonial Impediments of Consanguinity and Affinity, VI-125 pp., 1934.
91. White, Rev. Robert J., A.B., LL.B., S.T.B., J.C.D., Canonical Ante-Nuptial Promises and the Civil Law, VI-152 pp., 1934.
92. Herrera, Rev. Antonio Parra, O.C.D., J.C.D., Legislacion Ecclesiastica sobra el Ayuno y la Abstinencia, XI-191 pp., 1935.
93. Kennedy, Rev. Edwin J., J.C.D., The Special Matrimonial Process in Cases of Evident Nullity, X-165 pp., 1935.
94. Manning, Rev. John J., A.B., J.C.D., Presumption of Law in Matrimonial Procedure, XI-111 pp., 1935.
95. Moeder, Rev. John M., J.C.D., The Proper Bishop for Ordination and Dimissorial Letters, VII-135 pp., 1935.
96. O'Mara, Rev. William A., A.B., J.C.D., Canonical Causes for Matrimonial Dispensations, IX-155 pp., 1935.
97. Reilly, Rev. Peter, J.C.D., Residence of Pastors, IX-81 pp., 1935.
98. Smith, Rev. Mariner T., O.P., S.T.Lr., J.C.D., The Penal Law for Religious, VII-169 pp., 1935.
99. Whalen Rev. Donald W., A.M., J.C.D., The Value of Testimonial Evidence in Matrimonial Procedure, XIII-297 pp., 1935.
100. Cleary, Rev. Joseph F., J.C.D., Canonical Limitations on the Alienation of Church Property, VIII-141 pp., 1936.
101. Glynn, Rev. John C., J.C.D., The Promoter of Justice, XX-337 pp., 1936.
102. Brennan, Rev. James H., S.S., M.A., S.T.B., J.C.D., The Simple Convalidation of Marriage, VI-135 pp., 1937.
103. Brunini, Rev. Joseph Bernard, J.C.D., The Clerical Obligations of Canons 139 and 142, X-121 pp., 1937.
104. Connor, Rev. Maurice, A.B., J.C.D., The Administrative Removal of Pastors, VIII-159 pp., 1937.
105. Guilfoyle, Rev. Merlin Joseph, J.C.D., Custom, XI-144 pp., 1937.
106. Hughes, Rev. James Austin, A.B., A.M., J.C.D., Witnesses in Criminal Trials of Clerics, IX-140 pp., 1937.
107. Jansen, Rev. Raymond J., A.B., S.T.L., J.C.D., Canonical Provisions for Catechetical Instruction, VII-153 pp., 1937.
108. Kealy, Rev. John James, A.B., J.C.D., The Introductory Libellus in Church Court Procedure, XI-121 pp., 1937.
109. McManus, Rev. James Edward, C.SS.R., J.C.D., The Administration of Temporal Goods in Religious Institutes, XVI-196 pp., 1937.
110. Moriarity, Rev. Eugene James, J.C.D., Oaths in Ecclesiastical Courts, X-115 pp., 1937.
111. Rainier, Rev. Eligius George, C.SS.R., J.C.D., Suspension of Clerics, XVII-249 pp., 1937.

112. Reilly, Rev. Thomas F., C.SS.R., J.C.D., Visitation of Religious, VI-195 pp., 1938.
113. Moriarity, Rev. Francis E., C.SS.R., J.C.D., The Extraordinary Absolution from Censures, XV-334 pp., 1938.
114. Connolly, Rev. Nicholas P., J.C.D., The Canonical Erection of Parishes, X-132 pp., 1938.
115. Donovan, Rev. James Joseph, J.C.D., The Pastor's Obligation in Prenuptial Investigation, XII-322 pp., 1938.
116. Harrigan, Rev. Robert J., M.A., S.T.B. J.C.D., The Radical Sanation of Invalid Marriages, VIII-208 pp., 1938.
117. Boffa, Rev. Conrad Humbert, J.C.D., Canonical Provisions for Catholic Schools, VII-211 pp., 1939.
118. Parsons, Rev. Anscar John, O.M.Cap., J.C.D., Canonical Elections, XII-236 pp., 1939.
119. Reilly, Rev. Edward Michael, A.B., J.C.D., The General Norms of Dispensation, XII-156 pp., 1939.
120. Ryan, Rev. Gerald Aloysius, A.B., J.C.D., Principles of Episcopal Jurisdiction, XII-172 pp., 1939.
121. Burton, Rev. Francis James, C.S.C., A.B., J.C.D., A Commentary on Canon 1125, X-222 pp., 1940.
122. Miaskiewicz, Rev. Francis Sigismund, J.C.D., Supplied Jurisdiction According to Canon 209, XII-340 pp., 1940.
123. Rice, Rev. Patrick William, A.B., J.C.D., Proof of Death in Prenuptial Investigation, VIII-156 pp., 1940.
124. Anglin, Rev. Thomas Francis, M.S., J.C.D., The Eucharistic Fast, VIII-183 pp., 1941.
125. Coleman, Rev. John Jerome, J.C.D., The Minister of Confirmation, VI-153 pp., 1941.
126. Downs, Rev. John Emmanuel, A.B., J.C.D., The Concept of Clerical Immunity, XI-163 pp., 1941.
127. Esswein, Rev. Anthony Albert, J.C.D., Extrajudicial Penal Powers of Ecclesiastical Superiors, X-144 pp., 1941.
128. Farrell, Rev. Benjamin Francis, M.A., S.T.L., J.C.D., The Rights and Duties of the Local Ordinary Regarding Congregeations of Women Religious of Pontifical Approval, V-195 pp., 1941.
129. Feeney, Rev. Thomas John, A.B., S.T.L., J.C.D., Restitutio in Integrum, VI-169 pp., 1941.
130. Findley, Rev. Stephen William, O.S.B., A.B., J.C.D., Canonical Norms Governing the Deposition and Degradation of Clerics, XVII-279 pp., 1941.
131. Goodwine, Rev. John, A.B., S.T.L., J.C.D., The Right of the Church to Acquire Property, VIII-119 pp., 1941.
132. Heston, Rev. Edward Louis, C.S.C., Ph.D., S.T.D., J.C.D., The Alienation of Church Property in the United States, XII-222 pp., 1941.
133. Hogan, Rev. James John, A.B., S.T.L., J.C.D., Judicial Advocates and Procurators, XIII-200 pp., 1941.

134. KEALY, REV. THOMAS M., A.B., Litt.B., J.C.D., Dowry of Women Religious, IX-152 pp., 1941.
135. KEENE, REV. MICHAEL JAMES, O.S.B., J.C.D., Religious Ordinaries and Canon 198, V-164 pp., 1942.
136. KERIN, REV. CHARLES A., S.S., M.A., S.T.B., J.C.D., The Privation of Christian Burial, XVI-279 pp., 1941.
137. LOUIS, REV. WILLIAM FRANCIS, M.A., J.C.D., Diocesan Archives, X-101 pp., 1941.
138. MCDEVITT, REV. GILBERT JOSEPH, A.B., J.C.D., Legitimacy and Legitimation, X-247 pp., 1941.
139. MCDONOUGH, REV. THOMAS JOSEPH, A.B., J.C.D., Apostolic Administrators, X-217 pp., 1941.
140. MEIER, REV. CARL ANTHONY, A.B., J.C.D., Penal Administrative Procedure Against Negligent Pastors, XI-240 pp., 1941.
141. SCHMIDT, REV. JOHN ROGG, A.B., J.C.D., The Principles of Authentic Interpretation in Canon 17 of the Code of Canon Law, XII-331 pp., 1941.
142. SLAFKOSKY, REV. ANDREW LEONARD, A.B., J.C.D., The Canonical Episcopal Visitation of the Diocese, X-197 pp., 1941.
143. SWOBODA, REV. INNOCENT ROBERT, O.F.M., J.C.D., Ignorance in Relation to the Imputability of Delicts, IX-271 pp., 1941.
144. DUBÉ, REV. ARTHUR JOSEPH, A.B., J.C.D., The General Principles for the Reckoning of Time in Canon Law, VIII-299 pp., 1941.
145. MCBRIDE, REV. JAMES T., A.B., J.C.D., Incardination and Excardination of Seculars, XX-585 pp., 1941.
146. KRÓL, REV. JOHN T., J.C.D., The Defendant in Ecclesiastical Trials, XII-207 pp., 1942.
147. COMYNS, REV. JOSEPH J., C.SS.R., A.B., J.C.D., Papal and Episcopal Administration of Church Property, XIV-155 pp., 1942.
148. BARRY, REV. GARRETT FRANCIS, O.M.I., J.C.D., Violation of the Cloister, XII-260 pp., 1942.
149. BOLDUC, REV. GATIEN, C.S.V., A.B., S.T.L., J.C.D., Les Études dans les Religions Clèricales, VIII-155 pp., 1942.
150. BOYLE, REV. DAVID JOHN, M.A., J.C.D., The Juridic Effects of Moral Certitude on Pre-Nuptial Guarantees, XII-188 pp., 1942.
151. CANAVAN, REV. WALTER JOSEPH, M.A., LITT.D., J.C.D., The Profession of Faith, XII-143 pp., 1942.
152. DESROCHERS, REV. BRUNO, A.B., PH.L., S.T.B., J.C.D., Le Premier Concile Plènier de Québec et le Code de Droit Canonique, XIV-186 pp., 1942.
153. DILLON, REV. ROBERT EDWARD, A.B., J.C.D., Common Law Marriage, X-148 pp., 1942.
154. DODWELL, REV. EDWARD JOHN, PH.D., S.T.B., J.C.D., The Time and Place for the Celebration of Marriage, X-156 pp., 1942.
155. DONNELLAN, REV. THOMAS ANDREW, A.B., J.C.D., The Obligation of the Missa pro Populo, VII-131 pp., 1942.

156. Eltz, Rev. Louis Anthony, A.B., J.C.L., Cooperation in Crime.
157. Gass, Rev. Sylvester Francis, M.A., J.C.D., Ecclesiastical Pensions, XI-206 pp., 1942.
158. Guiniven, Rev. John Joseph, C.SS.R., J.C.D., The Precept of Hearing Mass, XIV-188 pp., 1942.
159. Gulczynski, Rev. John Theophilus, J.C.D., The Desecration and Violation of Churches, X-126 pp., 1942.
160. Hammill, Rev. John Leo, M.A., J.C.D., The Obligations of the Traveler According to Canon 14, VIII-204 pp., 1942.
161. Haydt, Rev. John Joseph, A.B., J.C.D., Reserved Benefices, XI-148 pp., 1942.
162. Huser, Rev. Roger John, O.F.M., A.B., J.C.D., The Crime of Abortion in Canon Law, XII-187 pp., 1942.
163. Kearney, Rev. Francis Patrick, A.B., S.T.L., J.C.L., The Principles of Canon 1127.
164. Linahen, Rev. Leo James, S.T.L., J.C.D., De Absolutione Complicis In Peccato Turpi, 114 pp., 1942.
165. McCloskey, Rev. Joseph Aloysius, A.B., J.C.D., The Subject of Ecclesiastical Law According to Canon 12, XVII-246 pp., 1942.
166. O'Neill, Rev. Francis Joseph, C.SS.R., J.C.D., The Dismissal of Religious in Temporary Vows, XIII-220 pp., 1942.
167. Prince, Rev. John Edward, A.B., S.T.B., J.C.D., The Diocesan Chancellor, X-136 pp., 1942.
168. Riesner, Rev. Albert Joseph, C.SS.R., J.C.D., Apostates and Fugitives from Religious Institutes, IX-168 pp., 1942.
169. Stenger, Rev. Joseph Bernard, J.C.D., The Mortgaging of Church Property, 186 pp., 1942.
170. Waldron, Rev. Joseph Francis, A.B., J.C.D., The Minister of Baptism, XII-197 pp., 1942.
171. Willett, Rev. Robert Albert, J.C.D., The Probative Value of Documents in Ecclesiastical Trials, X-124 pp., 1942.
172. Woeber, Rev. Edward Martin, M.A., J.C.D., The Interpellations, XII-161 pp., 1942.
173. Benko, Rev. Matthew Aloysius, O.S.B., M.A., J.C.D., The Abbot *Nullius*, XV-147 pp., 1943.
174. Christ, Rev. Joseph James, M.A., S.T.L., J.C.D., Dispensation from Vindicative Penalties, XIII-285 pp., 1943.
175. Clancy, Rev. Patrick M. J., O.P., A.B., S.T.Lr., J.C.D., The Local Religious Superior, X-229 pp., 1943.
176. Clarke, Rev. Thomas James, J.C.D., Parish Societies, XII-147 pp., 1943.
177. Connolly, Rev. John Patrick, S.T.L., J.C.D., Synodal Examiners and Parish Priest Consultors, X-223 pp., 1943.
178. Drumm, Rev. William Martin, A.B., J.C.L., Hospital Chaplains.
179. Flanagan, Rev. Bernard Joseph, A.B., S.T.L., J.C.D., The Canonical Erection of Religious Houses, X-147 pp., 1943.

180. KELLEHER, REV. STEPHEN JOSEPH, A.B., S.T.B., J.C.D., Discussions with non-Catholics: Canonical Legislation, X-93 pp., 1943.
181. LEWIS, REV. GORDIAN, C.P., J.C.D., Chapters in Religious Institutes, XII-169 pp., 1943.
182. MARX, REV. ADOLPH, J.C.L., The Declaration of Nullity of Marriages Contracted Outside the Church, X-151 pp., 1943.
183. MATULENAS, REV. RAYMOND ANTHONY, O.S.B., A.B., J.C.L., Communication, a Source of Privileges.
184. O'LEARY, REV. CHARLES GERARD, C.SS.R., J.C.D., Religious Dismissed After Perpetual Profession, X-213 pp., 1943.
185. POWER, REV. CORNELIUS MICHAEL, J.C.L., The Blessing of Cemeteries.
186. SHUHLER, REV. RALPH VINCENT, O.S.A., J.C.D., Privileges of Religious to Absolve and Dispense, XII-195 pp., 1943.
187. ZIOLKOWSKI, REV. THADDEUS STANISLAUS, A.B., J.C.L., The Consecration and Blessing of Churches, XII-151 pp., 1943.
188. HENEGHAN, REV. JOHN JOSEPH, S.T.D., J.C.L., The Marriages of Unworthy Catholics: Canons 1065 and 1066.
189. CARROLL, REV. COLEMAN FRANCIS, M.A., S.T.L., J.C.L., Charitable Institutions.
190. CIESLUK, REV. JOSEPH EDWARD, PH.B., S.T.L., J.C.L., National Parishes in the United States.
191. COBURN, REV. VINCENT PAUL, A.B., J.C.L., Marriages of Conscience.
192. CONNORS, REV. CHARLES PAUL, C.S.SP., A.B., J.C.L., Extra-Judicial Procurators in the Code of Canon Law.
193. COYLE, REV. PAUL RAYMOND, A.B., J.C.L., Judicial Exceptions.
194. FAIR, REV. BARTHOLOMEW FRANCIS, A.B., S.T.L., J.C.L., The Impediment of Abduction.
195. GALLAGHER, REV. THOMAS RAPHAEL, O.P., A.B., S.T.LR., J.C.L., The Examination of the Qualities of the Ordinand.
196. GANNON, REV. JOHN MARK, S.T.L., J.C.L., The Interstices Required for the Promotion to Orders.
197. GOLDSMITH, REV. J. WILLIAM, B.C.S. S.T.L., J.C.L., The Competence of Church and State over Marriage—Disputed Points.
198. GOODWINE, REV. JOSEPH GERARD, A.B., S.T.B., J.C.L., The Reception of Converts.
199. KOWALSKI, REV. ROMUALD EUGENE, O.F.M., A.B., J.C.L., Sustenance of Religious Houses of Regulars.
200. MCCOY, REV. ALAN EDWARD, O.F.M., J.C.L., Force and Fear in Relation to Delictual Imputability and Penal Responsibility.
201. MCDEVITT, REV. VINCENT JOHN, PH.B., S.T.L., J.C.L., Perjury.
202. MARTIN, REV. THOMAS OWEN, PH.D., S.T.D., J.C.L., Adverse Possession, Prescription and Limitation of Actions: The Canonical "Praescriptio."
203. MIKLOSOVIC, REV. PAUL JOHN, A.B., J.C.L., Attempted Marriages and Their Consequent Juridic Effects.

204. Mundy, Rev. Thomas Maurice, A.B., S.T.L., J.C.L., The Union of Parishes.
205. O'Day, Rev. John Coyle, A.B., J.C.L., The Matrimonial Impediment of Nonage.
206. Olalia, Rev. Alexander Ayson, S.T.L., J.C.L., A Comparative Study of the Christian Constitution of States and the Constitution of the Philippine Commonwealth.
207. Poisson, Rev. Pierre-Marie, C.S.C., A.B., Ph.L., Th.L., J.C.L., Droits Patrimoniaux des Maisons et des Églises Religieuses.
208. Stadalnikas, Rev. Casimir Joseph, M.I.C., J.C.L., Reservation of Censures.
209. Sullivan, Rev. Eugene Henry, S.T.L., J.C.L., Proof of the Reception of the Sacraments.
210. Vaughan, Rev. William Edward, J.C.L., Constitutions for Diocesan Courts.
211. Lyons, Rev. Joseph Henry, J.C.L., The Joinder of Issue in Canonical Trials.

www.ingramcontent.com/pod-product-compliance
Lightning Source LLC
LaVergne TN
LVHW050158080826
844660LV00012B/313

* 9 7 8 0 8 1 3 2 2 3 7 9 7 *